KETO

for the

Holidays

53 scrumptious, fat-burning recipes so you can thrive
on delicious KETO food through the Holidays

CARRIE BROWN

DEDICATION

Dr. Karen Ball

To the amazing lady that cured almost every ailment I've struggled with since childhood: I really don't know where I'd be today if it wasn't for your medical and naturopathic brilliance.

I am indebted to you for the quality of life that I enjoy today — and for the absence of prescription medications for which my bank balance is grateful beyond belief.

B vitamins, gluten, and those pesky serotonin and dopamine transmitters. Who knew?! You did.

THANK YOU. THANK YOU. THANK YOU.

ACKNOWLEDGMENTS

Brian Williamson – this book is entirely your fault. "You should make a Holiday Cookbook!" you said. So here we are. And you, Sir, are an outstanding human being who has willingly embraced the crazy that is Carrie Brown with unconditional support and wild abandon. I couldn't ask for a better partner in podcast crime.
For all that you are and all that you do – THANK YOU!

Rekka Jay – for your all round awesomeness in the graphic and proofing departments, I don't even have the words. THANK YOU!

Minta Hale – for taste testing like it was your job, for not caring about the state of my house during the writing of this book, and for being a constant source of support and encouragement – THANK YOU!

The Taste Test Crew – Sara Bush, Alisen Peterson, Scott Weiskopf, Mic Van Putten, Dawn Lee & the DisCo Posse, Rachael Jones, Ale Carneiro, Crystal Shelton, Abigail Wiechmann. Your endless enthusiasm for my grain-, gluten-, and sugar-free creations knows no bounds! For helping to make these recipes even better – THANK YOU!

Marc Levine – I reap the rewards of your incredible influence in my life Every. Single. Day.

You – if you bought this book, follow my blog, listen to our podcasts, or cheer from the sidelines on social media, you are the reason that I do what I do. Thank you for choosing the path to your health and wellness, and for being an important part of my world.

CONTENTS

IT'S THE HOLIDAYS! YAY?? YAY!!

For many of us, when we were growing up, the holidays were a time of absolute joy and wonder, and also involved consuming as much of some of our most favorite foods as we could cram into our little mouths. I know I looked forward to Christmas all year – more for the food than the presents. Christmas was the only time of the year that we had candy (sweets), chocolate cookies (biscuits), soda / pop (fizzy drinks), and chips (crisps). Plus, my mother rolled up her sleeves and cooked special Christmas fare like a mad woman for the two weeks prior. Christmas was truly magical in the food department at my childhood English home. I can still remember the waves of joy that Christmastime washed into my young life.

As we got older, the holidays may well have turned into half joy and half horror; 1. because of the amount of work involved, and 2. because of the probable consequences to our bodies and emotions from all the disastrous dietary options consumed.

And for everyone following a low-carb, KETO, or similarly healthy lifestyle and way of eating, the holidays have become something that a lot of us just dread. Can you say carb-fest?!

So when the ruggedly handsome Brian Williamson over at www.ketovangelist.com – my partner in low-carb and KETO crime – suggested that the world needed a Carrie Brown cookbook crammed full of delicious holiday recipes to save us from an overload of utter **carbage**, my recipe goals were thus:

- Ingredients that cause lower insulin and blood sugar responses.

- No grains, gluten, sugars, soy, or industrialized processed vegetable and seed oils.

- Nutrient dense ingredients.

- Simple – because no one needs complicated at the busiest time of the year.

- Easy – because everyone deserves to be able to create Holiday deliciousness.

- Fast – because delicious doesn't have to take hours or keep you in the kitchen forever.

- Delicious – if it ain't delicious then it's not good enough for you.

- Enough recipes to get you through the Holidays without having to spend hours trawling Pinterest or the internet for recipes which may or may not work, and may or may not be tasty.

- Your success in the kitchen – we all know that the internet and a lot of cookbooks are jammed with recipes that don't actually work. These waste your valuable time and money when they end up in the trash.

- Budget-friendly – I try to limit the number of strange or expensive ingredients to a minimum so that the recipes are affordable to as many people as possible, although there are some things that low-carb cooking requires for it to work.

With all this in mind, I came up with a bunch of recipes that make it possible for you to have a perfectly healthy and perfectly delicious holiday season without breaking the bank, taking up all your time and energy, without wasting any ingredients unnecessarily, and without causing you to gain ten pounds.

It's the holidays! YAY!!

~~~~~~

If you are new to my recipes then you may notice they're a bit different from most of the ones you're used to finding on the internet and in cookbooks, so here are a few notes of explanation:

- Precision – I am very precise and prescriptive in my recipes and there are really good reasons why. Those reasons typically revolve around it being easier for you to make, you having no production issues, and you getting a better final result. You are, of course, free to ignore my advice, but I cannot guarantee you will get great results if you do. I want you all to be able to find your inner Cooking Rockstar with these recipes.

- Where is it says "DO NOT USE XXXX" I highly recommend that you take heed, especially if it involves sweeteners. Alternative sweeteners do not behave like sugar, nor do they behave like each other, so I use different ones for different uses. Trust me on this one – I have gone through thousands of pounds of sweeteners and years of experimentation and recipe testing.

- I do not publish a recipe until it is perfect. If I am not 110% happy with the final result, or the method, or don't think it's replicable by everyone, I keep working on it until it is. Every recipe in this book has been tested and taste-tested rigorously.

- I weigh EVERYTHING. Weighing is the only way that you can guarantee consistently awesome results. This is why I do not give volume (cup) measurements for dry ingredients. For more information head, here: http://carriebrown.com/archives/27141

COOKING RESOURCES AND Q & A

I wanted this cookbook to be a simple collection of delicious holiday recipes, rather than a lengthy tome on the whys and wherefores of eating healthily with miles of information that you may or may not need, depending on where you are in your health journey. Because who has the time or inclination to sit down and wade through all that at this time of year, amongst all the happy holiday happenings and endless to-do lists? I figure that right now, all you really, really need is one place where you can get all the recipes that will have you sailing through the holidays with a happy heart, healthy body, and friends and family that will have no clue the food is free from grains, gluten, sugar, soy, and all that traditional *carbage*. (No, really. I taste tested these recipes with a bunch of unsuspecting people who did not know they were low-carb, as well as another bunch of people who are grain- and sugar-free. All of them said they couldn't tell they weren't made with traditional ingredients.)

However, I also get that some of you are new to this way of eating and all that involves. There's a few ingredients used here that might be strange to you. There's the odd piece of equipment you might not have come across before. But instead of including all that information in this cookbook along with all the delectable food, I'm including links to the information on my website instead, so if you need it you can easily grab it, and if you don't need it then you won't have to rifle through that info to get to the recipes.

And just in case you still have questions about ingredients, equipment, or recipes – after checking out the online info – there's a Q&A page for this cookbook on my website. Head there and see if the answer is already waiting for you. Feel free to add new questions in the comments and I will update the page with answers as they come in.

Now, let's get cooking!

INFORMATION ON INGREDIENTS
www.carriebrown.com/archives/23109

INFORMATION ON EQUIPMENT
www.carriebrown.com/archives/23310

KETO for the HOLIDAYS COOKBOOK Q&A
www.carriebrown.com/eat-smarter-holidays-cookbook-qa

BREAKFAST: Four Cheese Tarragon Sausage Casserole

Prep time: 20 mins | Cook time: 40 mins | Total time: 60 mins | Serves: 8

1 lb. / 450g ground pork (sausage meat)

1 lb. / 450g cream cheese

1 cup / 8 fl oz. chicken stock

1 ½ tsp. dried tarragon

Sea salt and black pepper to taste

18 slices thin sliced turkey

12 hardboiled eggs, finely chopped

6 oz. / 170g mozzarella, grated

2 oz. / 55g parmesan, finely grated

4 oz. / 110g Cheddar cheese, grated

Brown the sausage in a pan over medium heat, breaking up the meat into very small pieces as it cooks. When the meat has browned, add the cream cheese and chicken stock and stir well until completely combined. Stir in the tarragon and season with sea salt and pepper to taste.

Spray a casserole dish with coconut or avocado oil and spread a very thin layer of the sausage sauce in the bottom. Cover the sauce with a layer comprising of 6 slices of the turkey, and then spread half of the chopped hardboiled eggs evenly over the meat (like you were layering a lasagna).

Spread half of the mozzarella and half of the parmesan evenly over the layer of egg. Spread half of the sausage sauce evenly over the cheese.

Repeat the layers: 6 slices turkey, remainder of the chopped hardboiled eggs, remainder of the mozzarella and parmesan cheeses, remainder of the sausage sauce.

Layer the last 6 slices of turkey over the sausage sauce and spread the grated cheddar evenly over the top.

Bake in the center of the oven at 325°F for 40 minutes, until golden brown and bubbling.

~~~~~~

Top Tip: Cut through with a sharp knife before attempting to scoop out of the casserole dish.

You can assemble this several days in advance, cover tightly with plastic wrap & refrigerate. Remove wrap before baking, as melted plastic wrap is not a recommended topping.

BREAKFAST: Hot and Nutty Cereal

Prep time: 4 mins | Cook time: 1 min | Total time: 5 mins | Serves: 2

2 TBSP chia seeds

2 TBSP sunflower seeds

4 TBSP unsweetened coconut

2 TBSP ground flax seeds

4 TBSP almond meal

2 tsp pumpkin pie spice (or cinnamon if you don't have Pumpkin Pie Spice)

1 oz. / 30g vanilla protein powder of your choice

1 cup / 8 fl oz. boiling water

½ tsp vanilla extract

2 tsp xylitol or erythritol (or sweetener of choice)

Place chia seeds, sunflower seeds, and coconut in a coffee grinder and grind until fine. (If you use a blender such as a Vitamix, be careful you don't end up with a paste!)

Pour ground mix into a bowl, add ground flax seeds, almond meal, spice and vanilla whey powder. Mix well until completely blended.

Add cup of boiling water and stir well. Leave to sit for one minute to thicken.

Stir. Add more boiling water if you prefer a runnier cereal.

Add vanilla extract, and sweetener to taste, and serve with heavy cream if the mood takes you. Which it probably will.

~~~~~~

Love a big old bowl of steaming porridge in the morning? ME TOO. Except now I don't love the results of that particular carb-fest, so I came up with a most delicious alternative.

Top Tip: Make a large batch and keep it in the 'fridge so you have a jar of instant mix always ready to go. When I first dreamt up this recipe I was eating it every day. By bowl #5 I was already getting a bit jaded with the whole open-8-jars-and-scoop-stuff shenanigans, so I determined that what we ex-porridge-lovers needed was an instant version. Yes! Now I have a jar full of mix ready in the 'fridge and this Hot and Nutty Cereal has become the fastest route to a big bowl of warm, comforting low carb YUM. Head to http://carriebrown.com/archives/21240 for the bulk recipe. No math required!

BREAKFAST: Broccoli and Red Pepper Quiche Cups

Prep time: 10 mins | Cook time: 30 mins | Total time: 40 mins | Serves: 6

3 oz. / 85g red pepper, finely chopped

4 oz. / 110g broccoli, finely chopped

2 oz. / 55g sharp cheddar cheese, grated

11 eggs

¼ cup / 2 fl oz. Greek yogurt (Non-fat yogurt will not work!!)

1 tsp dried parsley

Sea salt and pepper to taste

Preheat oven to 375°F. Place 12 silicone cups in a muffin pan.

In a bowl combine red pepper, broccoli, and cheese, and mix well.

Divide vegetable and cheese mix evenly between the 12 silicone cups.

Place eggs, parsley, pepper, and Greek yogurt in a bowl and whisk well.

Pour egg mixture into a jug and carefully fill each silicone cup almost full.

Carefully place muffin pan into the center of the oven and bake for 30 minutes until risen, puffy and golden brown. They will rise well above the cups. They are ready when a skewer comes out cleanly.

Remove from oven and carefully tip each quiche out of the cups.

~~~~~~

Here's your party-in-a-muffin-cup perfect holiday breakfast! And just think: after the holidays are over and everyone around you is swilling down Slimfast and choking back fat-free 100-calorie snack packs, you'll still get to eat party food. Every. Single. Day. HURRAH!

Eat them on their own. Eat them hot for breakfast with some bacon. Or sausage. Eat them with a non-starchy veggie stir-fry for lunch. Eat them hot straight out of the oven or cold the next day. Make a big batch before the holidays begin and guests start arriving and have them ready to go in the 'fridge for the week. Eat them as a snack when you get the munchies. Take a big old pile on your next road trip for on-the-go goodness.

Just eat them. You'll love 'em.

BREAKFAST: Lemon Yogurt Supreme

Prep time: 5 mins | Cook time: 15 mins | Total time: 20 mins + chilling time

4 eggs

7 oz. / 195g xylitol (DO NOT USE ERYTHRITOL!)

⅓ cup / 2 ½ fl oz. lemon juice (approx. 2 lemons)

Zest of 1 lemon

4 oz. / 110g coconut oil, melted

4 oz. / 110g butter, melted

1 cup / 8 fl oz. unsweetened Greek yogurt

1 oz. / 28g vanilla protein powder of your choice

¼ tsp sea salt

Whisk the eggs well and pour into a small pan. Add the xylitol, lemon juice, lemon zest, coconut oil, and butter, and whisk well.

Place on the stove over a medium heat and STIR CONSTANTLY as the mixture slowly thickens. It takes 12 - 15 minutes to thicken fully. Embrace it. Be patient. Read a book. Meditate. Listen to our podcast.

DO NOT ALLOW THE MIXTURE TO BOIL – it will curdle or you will get scrambled eggs. Neither is desirable.

When the mixture is thick enough to coat the back of a spoon or spatula, quickly remove it from the heat and pour it through a fine mesh sieve into a clean glass lidded container (such as a Pyrex storage bowl). No, you cannot omit this step. It must be sieved! All hail the fine mesh sieve!

Stir the mixture in the sieve until you are left with only the zest pulp and a few strands of egg. You can use a second, clean spatula to scrape the underside of the sieve as you go.

Once all the curd has been passed through the sieve, leave it uncovered until completely cold, stirring every 10 minutes to prevent a skin from forming.

When cold, put the lid on the container and store in the 'fridge. Once chilled, it will be thick and spreadable. Plus, bright yellow and glorious.

Once the Lemon Curd is cold, stir the yogurt and ½ cup / 4 fl oz. Lemon Curd together in a bowl until completely mixed.

Add the protein powder and salt and mix well until the protein powder is completely dispersed and the yogurt is smooth and lump-free.

APPETIZER: Creamy Greek Cucumber Dip

Prep time: 10 mins | Cook time: 0 mins | Total time: 10 mins

2 oz. / 55g English cucumber

6 oz. / 170g Greek yogurt

1 tsp. lemon zest (about ½ a lemon)

½ tsp. dried dill

1 tsp. extra virgin olive oil

1 tsp. lemon juice

Sea salt and black pepper to taste

¼ cup / 2 fl oz. heavy cream, whipped

Put two joined pieces of paper towel on the counter and then put two more layers of paper towel on top of that so you have 3 layers of paper.

Using the smallest hole on your box grater, grate the cucumber onto the paper towel. Spread the grated cucumber out a bit and then roll up tightly in the kitchen paper. Unroll the paper and you should have mostly dry cucumber. If the cucumber is still wet, repeat with new paper.

Put the cucumber in a bowl and add the yogurt, lemon zest, dill, olive oil, lemon juice, sea salt, and black pepper and mix well with a whisk until completely combined. Lastly, stir in the whipped cream, cover, and refrigerate until required.

~~~~~~

Top Tip: Even if you got the cucumber very dry before making this dip you might find that it 'weeps' a little in the 'fridge, so stir well before serving. This can be made several days in advance and stored in the 'fridge – just remember the 'stirring well' part before serving.

I can't think of much that wouldn't be improved by dipping it in this. This dip is very light and refreshing with a bit of a tang. It's thin, yet creamy. A welcome contrast to all the holiday richness!

Dip your crisp, crunchy veggies, dip your crackers, dip your salami rolls and cold mini sausages. I even dipped a couple slices of Cheddar cheese, and I wouldn't be averse to dipping some chicken strips either. You could also use this as a delightful salad dressing. If you prefer a thinner dressing, whisk in some almond milk or thin coconut milk (from a carton) and then drizzle over your crisp salad greens. Makes me want to go make a salad *right now*. Even though it's the middle of a northern hemisphere Fall.

APPETIZER: Baked Cream Spinach Dip

Prep time: 10 mins | Cook time: 25 mins | Total time: 35 mins

1 cup / 8 fl oz. unsweetened mayonnaise

2 oz. / 55g parmesan, finely grated

4 oz. / 110g cream cheese, softened

8 oz. / 225g frozen spinach, thawed and drained

1 can of artichoke hearts, drained well

4 oz. / 110g red pepper, finely chopped

1 TBSP nutritional yeast

½ tsp. lemon pepper

2 ½ oz. / 70g mozzarella, grated

Preheat oven to 350°F. Spray a casserole dish with coconut or avocado oil.

Place the mayonnaise, parmesan, and softened cream cheese in a bowl and beat well until completely combined.

Finely chop the thawed, drained spinach and the drained artichoke hearts. Add to the mayonnaise mixture and stir well. Add ¾ of the chopped red pepper, the nutritional yeast, and the lemon pepper, and stir well.

Spread the mixture in the casserole dish, and then spread the grated mozzarella and the remaining ¼ of the chopped red pepper evenly over the surface.

Cover the casserole with foil and bake for 15 minutes. Carefully remove the foil and continue baking for another 10 minutes.

Serve warm, or leave to cool completely before covering with plastic wrap and storing in the 'fridge.

~~~~~~

Top Tip: When looking for mayonnaise, pick one that is made with avocado, olive, or another healthy oil. Steer clear of canola, sunflower, safflower, soy, or any other processed, industrial seed or vegetable oils. Minimally processed oils from fruits and nuts for the win!

Make this awesome dip several days in advance, and either serve cold or gently reheat.

As well as a fantastic holiday appetizer to scoop up with crackers, this would be great as a side dish to a lovely piece of poached salmon, pan-fried chicken pieces (skin on!), or juicy pork chops.

APPETIZER: Smoky Bacon and Tomato Dip

Prep time: 10 mins | Cook time: 10 mins | Total time: 20 mins

1 cup / 8 fl oz. unsweetened mayonnaise

1 cup / 8 fl oz. sour cream

8 oz. / 225g cream cheese

2 oz. / 55g Cheddar cheese, grated

12 oz. / 340g tomatoes, finely chopped and well drained

12 oz. / 340g bacon, cooked and chopped into small pieces

3 oz. / 85g green onions (spring onions), finely chopped

1 tsp. smoked paprika

Sea salt and black pepper to taste

Place the mayonnaise, sour cream, and cream cheese in a pan and heat gently, stirring constantly, until the cream cheese is melted and they are all completely combined.

Remove from the heat, add the grated Cheddar cheese, and stir until the cheese has melted.

Add the chopped drained tomatoes, cooked chopped bacon, and chopped green onions. Stir well.

Add the smoked paprika, sea salt and black pepper to taste and stir well.

Serve warm or leave to cool completely before covering with plastic wrap and storing in the 'fridge.

~~~~~~

Top Tip: Do not over heat this dip as the Cheddar cheese will become oily and form puddles on the surface. It will still taste fantastic but will be very ugly. Not what we want on our holiday table.

This can be made several days in advance and either served cold or gently reheated.

Aside from making a winning dip for your holiday gatherings, this Smoky Bacon and Tomato yum would be great served warm as a sauce over a pan-fried boneless pork chop on a bed of cauliflower rice. Thinking about it, that wouldn't just be great, that would be stinkin' awesome.

You could also make yourself a BLT by rolling up spoonfuls of cold dip in some romaine or butter lettuce leaves for lunch. Or split an almond flour biscuit in half and pile this on top for a delicious open sandwich. Smoky Bacon and Tomato Dip – it's not just for dipping!

APPETIZER: Creamy Salmon and Chive Dip

Prep time: 10 mins | Cook time: 0 mins | Total time: 10 mins

1 × 15 oz. / 420g can salmon, drained

8 oz. / 225g cream cheese, softened

3 TBSP lemon juice

½ oz. / 15g chives, finely chopped

Black pepper to taste

Place the drained salmon and softened cream cheese in a bowl and beat well until they are completely combined. This takes a few minutes and a bit of arm work.

Add the lemon juice, chopped chives, and black pepper. Mix well.

~~~~~~

Top Tip: If you wish, you can remove the skin and bones from the salmon before you mix it with the cream cheese. However, you will have no clue they are in there by the time you've finished beating the dip together, so I recommend just leaving them in. Think about all that extra nutritious goodness!

This dip can be made several days in advance, covered tightly with plastic wrap, and either served cold straight from the 'fridge or brought up to room temperature before serving if you prefer a softer consistency.

Of course, you can use whatever you fancy to shovel your dip with, but my very favorite things to use as a dip transporter for this bowl of salmon-y scrumptiousness are fresh cucumber slices. In my estimation, this dense and sturdy dip does well with the light, refreshing bite of cucumber.

Maybe it's because I'm British and grew up on salmon and cucumber sandwiches, but salmon and cucumber has always been a magical combination to my taste buds. It helped that my father was the Cucumber King and grew cucumbers in a greenhouse at the bottom of our garden faster than we could eat them. I spent my childhood eating cucumbers fresh off the vine like they were apples. This was part of our solution to the vast over-population of cucumbers threatening to bury us alive in our kitchen on a weekly basis.

If you dip with cucumbers and you live in America, I urge you to head for the English cucumbers instead of the regular ones. Why? English cucumbers don't have the tough, bitter skin of their American cousins, being blessed instead with a skin that is easy to eat and cut and much sweeter to the taste. No more cucumber peeling required! The other noticeable difference is the absence of the large, sometimes hard seeds that American cucumbers tote around. GO, English!

APPETIZER: Sausage Stuffed Mushrooms

Prep time: 10 mins | Cook time: 40 mins | Total time: 50 mins | Serves 6 - 12

6 oz. / 170g ground pork (sausage meat)

4 oz. / 110g cauliflower rice (cauliflower processed to resemble rice)

2 oz. / 55g cream cheese

1 oz. / 30g parmesan, grated

1 oz. / 30g pine nuts

1 ½ tsp. dried thyme

12 large mushrooms, stems removed

1 egg

Preheat oven to 375°F. Spray a casserole dish with coconut or avocado oil and place the mushrooms (stems removed) upside-down in the dish.

Cook the sausage in a pan over medium heat, breaking up the meat into very small pieces as it cooks. Once the sausage is no longer pink, add the riced cauliflower and stir well. Continue cooking, stirring frequently until the cauliflower is soft – about 10 minutes.

Add the cream cheese and stir well until completely melted and then remove the pan from the heat. Add the parmesan, pine nuts, and dried thyme. Mix well and allow to cool.

Beat the egg and then add to the cooled sausage mixture and mix well. Using a small spoon, divide the sausage mixture between the upturned mushrooms. Use your fingers to form domes of stuffing.

Bake in the center of the oven for 20 minutes until the pine nuts are nicely browned.

~~~~~~

Top Tip: Use white mushrooms instead of Cremini mushrooms if you whiter mushroom cups.

This stuffing is made possible by the perennial low-carber's favorite vegetable, the humble cauliflower, in place of the breadcrumbs. If you don't tell your non-low-carb guests it's cauliflower they'll be none the wiser, but their bodies will secretly be thanking you.

Increasingly, you can buy cauliflower rice ready-made in grocery stores, but it's easy enough to make yourself by pulsing cauliflower florets for a few seconds in a food processor until it resembles rice. If you value time over money, grab bags of the cauliflower rice and lob them in the freezer. If you value money over time, grab some heads of cauliflower, process them into rice, and then freeze in 1 lb. bags.

APPETIZER: Mini Pizza Pies

Prep time: 15 mins | Cook time: 40 mins | Total time: 55 mins | Serves 9 - 18

1 TBSP coconut or avocado oil

1 lb. / 450g cauliflower rice (cauliflower processed to resemble rice)

2 oz. / 55g parmesan, grated

1 tsp. dried Italian seasoning

1 egg, beaten

½ cup / 4 fl oz. unsweetened tomato sauce / marinara sauce

2 ½ oz. / 70g mozzarella, grated

2 ½ oz. / 70g Cheddar cheese, grated

3 oz. / 85g salami, sliced into small pieces

Preheat oven to 400°F. Spray 18 silicone muffin cups or 2 muffin pans with coconut oil.

Heat the oil over a medium heat and add the cauliflower rice. Cook the cauliflower, stirring frequently, for 10 minutes. Remove from the heat and leave to cool slightly.

Add the parmesan, Italian seasoning, and beaten egg to the cooled cauliflower rice and mix well.

Divide the cauliflower mixture amongst 18 muffin cups using a small spoon.

Using your thumbs, push the cauliflower mixture gently up the sides of the muffin cups to form a well in the center.

Bake in the center of the oven for 20 minutes, until just starting to brown.

Carefully remove from the oven and spoon a little tomato sauce into the center of each cauliflower cup.

Mix the grated cheeses together and sprinkle evenly over top of the tomato sauce in each cup.

Divide the pieces of chopped salami evenly over the cheese.

Return to the oven and bake for a further 10 minutes until the cheese has fully melted and the salami is starting to crisp.

~~~~~~

Top Tip: Try not to inhale all 18 of these within 15 minutes of removing them from the oven. I bet you'll want to.

APPETIZER: Mini Cheese and Leek Quiches

Prep time: 15 mins | Cook time: 35 mins | Total time: 50 mins | Serves 12

6 ¾ oz. / 190g almond flour (ground almonds)

½ tsp sea salt

2 tsp xanthan gum

1 ½ oz. / 40g cold butter, chopped into small pieces

1 ½ oz. / 40g strong cheddar cheese, finely grated

¼ cup / 2 fl oz. heavy cream

1 TBSP coconut or avocado oil

7 oz. / 170g leeks, finely chopped

4 eggs

1½ TBSP heavy cream

½ tsp celery salt

Ground black pepper

Preheat oven to 375°F.

Put the almond flour, sea salt, xanthan gum, and butter in a food processor and pulse until it resembles fine breadcrumbs. Turn into a bowl and mix in the cheese until evenly distributed. Add the ¼ cup / 2 fl oz. cream and mix well to form a dough. Knead the dough lightly until smooth.

Roll out the dough to ¼" thick and cut out circles using a 3" round cutter. Gather up the trimmings into a ball, re-roll, and cut remaining dough into rounds. Very carefully, slide each dough circle into a muffin pan and gently push down to form dough cups. Not going to lie – the dough is delicate and a little tricky. Patience is required!

Heat the oil over a medium heat, add the leeks, and sauté until soft. Remove from the heat and divide the leeks evenly between the 12 dough cups in the muffin pan.

In a jug, whisk together the eggs, 1½ TBSP cream, celery salt, and black pepper really well. Carefully pour the egg mixture evenly between the 12 quiches.

Very carefully transfer the muffin pan to the center of the oven and bake for 25 minutes until the crust is brown and the egg is puffy and set.

(If you do not have the time or inclination for the crust, just fill muffin cups with the leeks, 4 oz. / 110g grated Cheddar, and the egg mixture. Bake directly in the muffin cups for crustless quiches).

APPETIZER: Parmesan Zucchini Strips

Prep time: 5 mins | Cook time: 13 mins | Total time: 18 mins | Serves 10 - 20

3 large zucchini (courgettes)

Avocado Oil

Dried thyme

Parmesan cheese, finely grated

Preheat oven to 400°F.

Slice the zucchini diagonally in ¼" thick slices (see picture).

Place the zucchini strips on a cooling rack over a sheet of baking parchment on your counter.

Brush the upper side of each zucchini strip with avocado oil using a pastry brush.

Sprinkle the parmesan liberally over the zucchini strips. The excess parmesan will fall onto the parchment below.

Lift the cooling rack off the parchment paper and place to one side. Pour the parmesan on the parchment paper carefully back into the cheese container for future use.

Sprinkle dried thyme over the zucchini strips. Place the cooling rack directly onto the shelf in the center of the oven.

Bake for 13 minutes until they are golden brown.

~~~~~~

Top Tip: Baking them directly on a cooling rack on the oven shelf helps to draw out moisture from the zucchini and prevent them from being soggy. They do soften over time once cooked, so serving them soon after baking is best. They're still good cold the next day, albeit a little softer.

I've secretly never thought zucchini – courgettes, as they're known in England – were very exciting vegetables, although Americans go wild for the things, especially in the Fall. However, I've discovered that if I douse them in cheese and bake them in the oven, they're pretty much my favorite thing on Earth, at least for the 10 minutes that I'm eating them.

I used parmesan to make veggies more exciting while writing my KETO Sides and Salads Cookbook (http://carriebrown.com/keto-sides-salads-cookbook). I wanted to make eggplant awesome, and it turns out that parmesan cheese makes eggplant more exciting than you thought it was possible for an eggplant to be. These Parmesan Zucchini Strips are very different, but parmesan definitely elevates zucchini into something quite fantastic.

APPETIZER: Mozzarella Tomato Basil Canapes

Prep time: 15 mins | Cook time: 22 mins | Total time: 37 mins | Serves 16 - 24

7 oz. / 195g almond flour (ground almonds)

½ oz. / 15g coconut flour

1 tsp. xanthan gum

4 tsp. baking powder

1 oz. / 30g parmesan, finely grated

2 oz. / 55g butter, cold

1 egg, beaten

16 – 24 large fresh basil leaves

8 oz. / 225g block mozzarella for slicing

16 - 24 cherry tomatoes

Preheat oven to 325°F.

Put the almond flour, coconut flour, xanthan gum, baking powder, and parmesan in a food processor and pulse briefly to mix. Chop the cold butter into small pieces and add to the dry ingredients in the food processor. Pulse until the ingredients resemble fine breadcrumbs.

Turn the mixture into a bowl, add the beaten egg, and mix into a dough. Knead lightly just until the dough is formed.

Roll out the dough to ¼" thick and cut out biscuits using whatever fancy holiday cutter floats your boat. Or use a round one. Or a flower one like I did. Just do you.

Using a palette knife carefully lift the biscuits onto a baking sheet sprayed with coconut oil. Re-roll the scraps and cut more biscuits until the dough is all gone.

Prick each biscuit a few times with a fork and bake in the center of the oven for 22 minutes until browned. Cool completely on a cooling rack before storing in an airtight container.

Just before serving, slice the mozzarella and tomatoes, place a basil leaf on each biscuit, followed by a slice of mozzarella and the tomato.

~~~~~~

My friends, Larry and Sue, always served mozzarella and tomato slices with basil atop toasted French bread. They were my favorite so I decided to create a sturdy biscuit base to transport the MTB goodness into my gob without all the floury, gluten-y yuck being involved. Voila!

APPETIZER: Cheddar Chive Crackers

Prep time: 15 mins | Cook time: 28 mins | Total time: 42 mins

7 oz. / 195g almond flour (ground almonds)

½ oz. / 15g nutritional yeast

¼ tsp. baking powder

½ tsp. sea salt

½ oz. / 15g fresh chives, finely chopped

4 oz. / 110g Cheddar cheese, grated

1 oz. / 30g butter

2 eggs

Preheat oven to 350°F.

Put the almond flour, nutritional yeast, baking powder, sea salt, chopped chives, and grated cheese in a bowl and mix well.

Melt the butter in a small bowl in the microwave or over a very low heat in a pan. Add the eggs and whisk to combine. Pour the egg mixture into the dry ingredients and mix into a dough. Let the dough rest for 10 minutes so that it's easier to handle.

Once rested, place the dough on a large piece of parchment paper and flatten with your hands. Lay a second piece of parchment paper on top of the dough and then roll the dough out between the two sheets of parchment until it is no more than ¼" thick (see picture).

Lift off the top piece of parchment and cut out crackers using a small round cutter, but do not try to move the crackers from the parchment. Instead, lift the scraps that are between the crackers off the parchment. When the scraps are all removed, leaving you with your crackers on the parchment, lift the parchment onto a baking sheet. Make a second tray with the scraps by repeating the process. Prick the crackers with a fork.

Bake in the center of the oven for 28 - 30 minutes, or until golden brown. Do not be tempted to take them out too soon or they will be soft. Longer is better as long as they don't burn. Burning = no bueno. Leave to cool on the baking sheet. When cold, store in an airtight container.

~~~~~~

Top Tip: these crackers are much better when cold – they get crisper and crunchier as they cool. Resist the temptation to chow down on them all when you pull them out of the oven! I know you'll want to. Public Health Warning: These crackers may make you insanely happy.

APPETIZER: Almond Crunch Crackers

Prep time: 15 mins | Cook time: 26 mins | Total time: 41 mins

6 oz. / 170g almond meal (ground almonds with the skins on)

1 tsp. onion powder

1 tsp. sea salt

2 egg whites

Preheat oven to 350°F.

Put the almond flour, onion powder, and sea salt into a bowl and mix well. Add the egg whites and mix into a dough.

Place the dough on a large piece of parchment paper and flatten with your hands. Lay a second piece of parchment paper on top of the dough and then roll the dough out between the two sheets of parchment until it is very thin – ⅛" thick (see picture). They do not rise, so roll them the thickness of the baked cracker. Try to roll the dough as close to a rectangle or square shape as you can.

Lift off the top piece of parchment and, using a ruler as a guide, cut the dough into squares with a pizza cutter or sharp knife, without moving or separating any of the crackers. You will end up with a sheet of dough scored into squares. Remove any rough edges and incomplete squares from the outside edges of the piece of dough. Or leave them on there and plan to eat those as samples. ☺

Bake in the center of the oven for 13 minutes. Carefully remove the tray from the oven and gently break the sheet up into the individual crackers that you cut before they went in the oven. Turn all the crackers over on the tray so the bottoms of the crackers are now facing upwards. Return tray to the oven and bake for another 13 minutes until the crackers are golden brown.

For the last few minutes, keep a close eye on them to make sure they don't burn, but do not be tempted to take them out too soon if you want crunchy crackers. Longer is better, as long as they don't burn. No one likes burnt crackers. No one. Leave to cool on the baking sheet. When completely cold store in an airtight container.

~~~~~~

Top Tip: Patience is a virtue with these crackers. 13 minutes each side feels like a lifetime. Let the color be your guide and trust me when I tell you they are so worth the wait.

I was so *wildly* excited about these crackers I forgot to count them, and then I ate them all so I couldn't. I also don't know if they freeze well, because, well, there were none to freeze. Sorry.

ENTREE: Roast Turkey

Every time I cook a whole roast turkey, everyone begs me to tell them how I get a turkey so moist and delicious. One year, a neighbor even persuaded me to roast their turkey for them on Thanksgiving Day and deliver it half an hour before dinner. So I thought it was about time I documented what I do and share it with the world. There is no picture because I am certain that you all know what a roasted turkey looks like.

Turkey

2 lbs. / 900g oranges

Avocado oil

Don't forget to defrost your turkey several days ahead of time if you bought a frozen one. You can accelerate thawing by placing the still-wrapped turkey in a sink full of room temperature water which you change out every few hours. One thawed, store in the 'fridge on a rimmed baking sheet to catch any drips. You don't want to have to clean the 'fridge out the day before Thanksgiving or Christmas.

Unwrap the turkey and pull out all little bags of *bits and pieces* you'll find therein. DO NOT DISCARD THEM! They make the best gravy, ever. Trust me on this. Make sure you also remove any plastic or other materials that may have been used to package the turkey with.

Wash all the cavities out thoroughly with water. I typically position my turkey under the tap and flush it out that way. If it's a big bird then be careful as wet turkeys can be slippery suckers.

Pat all the surfaces of the turkey – inside and out – as dry as you can with paper towels.

Most birds are big enough that you are going to have to make a super-sized piece of foil to wrap it in. Here's how you do that:

- Cut two long, equal length pieces of foil off the roll (each at least 12 inches longer than your turkey).

- Lay one piece of foil on top of the other with the shiny sides together.

- Take one long side and carefully fold both pieces of foil over together tightly a few times to form a seam. Flatten the seam well so it is secure.

- Turn the foil over and open the two pieces out so the shiny side is on the bottom and the dull side facing up. You should now have one huge piece of foil with a seam down the middle.

Place your dry turkey in the middle of your foil.

Quarter all the oranges and stuff both ends of the turkey with them. Just crush them in there! You're not going to eat the oranges so you don't need to worry about how they look.

'Stitch' up the openings with cooking twine (or use toothpicks (cocktail sticks) to hold the skin together).

Now comes the fun part. Using your hands, rub avocado oil liberally over all surfaces of your turkey. If you have a really huge bird, you might like to get some assistance with this as the bird will be seriously slippery and may try to escape your clutches.

Once your turkey is all oiled up, place it in the center of the foil and wrap it like a parcel by bringing the two edges of foil together over the turkey, folding them together to make a seam and then folding the ends up so that the turkey is completely enclosed in foil.

Carefully (so you don't tear the foil) pick up your foiled turkey and place it on a rack in your roasting pan, or even better (if you have one), a covered oval roaster with roasting rack. Using a rack makes it a lot easier to get the juices for the gravy.

Place the roasting pan with your turkey in the oven and also place an oven-proof dish or tin filled with water on the bottom rack of your oven. Do not omit the container of water in the bottom of the oven!

Cook your turkey according to the following chart:

Oven-ready weight	Hours at 450°F
6 - 8 lb. / 2.7 - 3.6 kg	2 ¼ - 2 ½
8 - 10 lb. / 3.6 - 4.5 kg	2 ½ - 2 ¾
10 - 12 lb. / 4.5 - 5.4 kg	2 ¾
12 - 14 lb. / 5.4 - 6.3 kg	3
14 - 16 lb. / 6.3 - 7.3 kg	3 - 3 ¼
16 - 18 lb. / 7.3 - 8.2 kg	3 ¼ - 3 ½
18 - 20 lb. / 8.2 - 9 kg	3 ½ - 3 ¾
20 - 22 lb. / 9 - 10 kg	3 ¾ - 4

Some of you may be looking at that chart and going, "Wait. What?! But turkeys take forever and I have to get up at the crack of dawn to get that thing in the oven."

No, no you don't. You can roast a turkey perfectly in a few hours if you cook it at a high temperature, and I promise you it will be as juicy as all get out. I've done it countless times over the last 25 years and have made fans every time someone has eaten one of my roast turkeys.

Half an hour before the end of the roasting time, carefully pull the turkey out and open the foil. Be very careful as a lot of steam will come rushing out at you. Fold the foil back on each side to expose the breast and legs so that they can brown and crisp.

At the end of the cooking time, remove the turkey from the oven and close the foil back up until you are ready to carve and serve your deliciously juicy bird which will be delicately scented with orange.

The oranges, oil, foil, covered roasting pan, and container of water in the bottom of the oven all create steam for your turkey to luxuriate in, and that along with the high heat / fast cooking time is why you will be eating the juiciest turkey you've ever had. Gobble, gobble!

ENTREE: Turkey & Cranberry Meatloaf

Prep time: 20 mins | Cook time: 1 hour | Total time: 1 hour 20 mins | Serves: 8

1 TBSP coconut or avocado oil

4 large stalks celery, finely chopped

1 lb. / 450g leeks, finely chopped

3 oz. / 85g dried unsweetened cranberries

2 TBSP finely chopped fresh sage

2 tsp salt

1 tsp ground black pepper

2 tsp xanthan gum

8 oz. / 225g almond meal (with skins on)

3 TBSP egg white (from 1 large egg or 2 small eggs)

2 lb. / 900g ground (minced) turkey

½ cup whole berry Cranberry Sauce (page 65)

Preheat oven to 350°F. Spray a loaf pan with coconut or avocado oil.

Heat the oil in a pan and sauté the vegetables over medium heat, stirring regularly, until the moisture has all been cooked out. About 15 minutes.

Meanwhile, in a large mixing bowl, put the dried cranberries, sage, salt, pepper, xanthan gum, and almond meal, and mix well until completely combined. Once the vegetables are ready, add into the mixing bowl with the dry ingredients.

Add the egg white and ground turkey and stir well. Hands are the best tool here, although the mixture is a little sticky. Turn the meat mixture into the loaf pan, and press into all corners and sides.

Bake meatloaf in center of oven for an hour. Remove from oven and let rest for 10 minutes.

Slide a knife around the edges of the meatloaf to make sure the sides are free. Take a cooling rack and place on top of the meatloaf in the pan. Carefully turn the cooling rack and pan over and the meatloaf will slide out. It may need a little shake.

Spread whole berry cranberry sauce on the top surface of the loaf before serving.

~~~~~~

Fantastic hot, glorious cold. Also slices like a dream for a perfect packed lunch.

ENTREE: Creamy Basil Chicken Marsala

Prep time: 5 mins | Cook time: 5 hours + 10 mins | Total time: 5 hours + 15 mins | Serves 4

8 skin-on, bone-in chicken thighs

Sea salt and ground black pepper

5 oz. / 140g wild mushrooms (whatever kind of wild you fancy), chopped

¾ cup / 6 fl oz. Marsala cooking wine

¼ cup / 2 fl oz. chicken stock

½ cup / 8 fl oz. heavy cream

2 tsp. erythritol

1 tsp. sea salt

1 ½ tsp. konjac flour / glucomannan powder

8 large fresh basil leaves, shredded

Sprinkle sea salt and black pepper on the skin of the chicken thighs and then put them **skin side down** in a pan over high heat. You're not trying to cook the chicken, you're only crisping and browning that gorgeous skin, so fast and furious in the frying pan is what we need. You do not need to turn and cook the other side. This will only take a few minutes.

Once the skin is golden and crisp, use tongs and carefully place the chicken pieces **skin side up** in a single layer in your slow cooker. Scatter the chopped mushrooms over the chicken and then pour the Marsala and chicken stock over the top. Cover and cook on low for 5 hours.

Carefully remove the chicken pieces from the slow cooker and place in a serving dish, skin side up, and then turn the slow cooker to high and add the cream.

Into a small dish measure the erythritol, sea salt, and konjac flour and mix well.

While whisking the liquid in the slow cooker rapidly with one hand, gently and slowly shake the konjac flour mixture into the liquid with the other hand. Whisk well for 2 minutes as the sauce thickens. Once the sauce has thickened, stir in the fresh basil and pour the sauce over the chicken.

~~~~~~

Top Tip: Go gently and slowly when adding the konjac flour mixture, otherwise you will end up with a clumpy sauce. I can't think of one instance when a clumpy sauce is a good thing. Not one.

Your '15-minutes-of-effort-but-completely-wow-the-pants-off-your-guests' entree. You're welcome.

ENTREE: Boozy Braised Beef Short Ribs

Prep time: 10 mins | Cook time: 7 hours + 10 mins | Total time: 7 hours + 20 mins | Serves 4

3 lb. / 1350g beef short ribs

Sea salt and ground black pepper

3 cloves garlic, crushed

1 jar unsweetened tomato / marinara sauce

2 TBSP erythritol

2 TBSP coconut aminos

1 cup / 8 fl oz. beef stock

1 cup / 8 fl oz. Marsala cooking wine

½ tsp. konjac flour / glucomannan powder

Place the short ribs in a pan over high heat and season with sea salt and ground black pepper. Using tongs, quickly sear and brown all sides of the ribs and then carefully place them in your slow cooker.

Put the crushed garlic in the pan you used to brown the beef and sauté over medium heat until just starting to brown. Add the tomato / marinara sauce, erythritol, coconut aminos, beef stock, and Marsala to the pan. Stir well and bring just to the boil. Carefully pour the hot sauce into the slow cooker with the ribs, cover, and cook on low for 7 hours.

Very carefully, lift the ribs out of the slow cooker and place on a serving dish and turn the slow cooker to high.

While whisking the liquid in the slow cooker rapidly with one hand, gently and slowly shake the konjac flour into the liquid with the other hand. Whisk well for 2 minutes as the sauce thickens.

Spoon the sauce over the ribs and serve.

~~~~~~

Top Tip: Go gently and slowly when adding the konjac flour, otherwise you will end up with a clumpy sauce. Who likes a clumpy sauce? *No one raised their hand*.

These ribs are meltingly soft, fall-off-the-bone tender. Now, I never met a beef short rib that I didn't like, but this recipe elevated them to the love level in very short order.

Bonus: short ribs are the fattiest cut of beef (Mmmmm! Flavor!) but also one of the cheapest.

ENTREE: Roasted Salmon with Avocado Salsa

Prep time: 10 mins | Cook time: 12 mins | Total time: 22 mins | Serves: 4

4 salmon filets

2 oz. / 55g butter

Sea salt and ground black pepper

2 tsp. ground cumin

2 TBSP avocado oil

3 tsp. erythritol

½ tsp. sea salt

¼ cup lime juice

1 avocado

2 TBSP finely chopped fresh cilantro (coriander)

2 oz. / 55g onion, finely chopped

Preheat oven to 475°F.

Put butter on a rimmed cookie sheet and place in the center of the oven for 1 minute just until the butter melts. Carefully remove the sheet from the oven. Don't forget the oven gloves.

Season the top of each salmon filet evenly with sea salt, ground black pepper, and ground cumin. Using a spatula, carefully slide each fillet – skin side down – into the melted butter and then return the sheet to the oven. Roast the salmon until just cooked – about 8 - 12 minutes depending on how thick your fillets are. The salmon will flake easily when cooked.

Meanwhile, put the avocado oil, erythritol, sea salt, and lime juice into a bowl and whisk well.

Cut the avocado in half lengthwise and remove the stone. Peel each avocado half and slice the avocado lengthwise and then widthwise to get small pieces (see picture). Add the avocado, finely chopped cilantro, and finely chopped onion to the bowl with the lime and oil mixture and stir until all the avocado is coated with liquid.

Lift the salmon filets carefully from the cookie sheet and place on plates. Spoon ¼ of the avocado salsa onto each filet, garnish with sprigs of fresh cilantro (coriander) and serve.

~~~~~~

Top Tip: The salsa can be made well in advance and stored, tightly covered, in the 'fridge. Then, this gorgeous dinner will be ready in the time it takes the salmon to roast. It's also very lovely served cold.

SIDE DISH: Cream of Mushroom Soup

Prep time: 10 mins | Cook time: 10 mins | Total time: 20mins | Serves: 4 - 6

2 TBSP coconut oil

6 cloves garlic, crushed

1 ½ lb. / 670g mushrooms

3 cups / 1 ½ pints beef stock

½ cup / 4 fl oz. heavy (double) cream

1 tsp. sea salt

1 tsp. guar gum

Heat the coconut oil in a pan over medium heat, add the crushed garlic and sauté until soft, but not browned. Add the mushrooms, lower the heat, and sweat for 5 minutes. Add the stock and bring to boil.

Using a slotted spoon, carefully remove half the mushrooms into a bowl and reserve.

Transfer the remaining mushrooms and stock to the blender, add the cream and sea salt, and blend like mad until smooth.

Turn the blender to low, and slowly tap the guar gum through the opening in the lid.

Add the reserved mushrooms and pulse a few times on the lowest possible speed to keep the mushrooms with a lot of texture. Warm gently if necessary.

~~~~~~

I have a love for mushrooms that runs very, very deep. In my little world, much like bacon, mushrooms make everything better. Except maybe oatmeal, but since I no longer eat oats, it's really not a problem of any great magnitude.

The best Mushroom Soup I've ever had the pleasure of slurping down was in Jukkasjärvi, Swedish Lapland, way up there in the Arctic Circle. I cannot imagine where they got mushrooms in the middle of a -40 °C winter, but they sure knew what to do with them once they got their mitts on some. My eyes flew open as wide as saucers the moment the first spoonful slipped past my lips. I could have eaten that soup every day for the rest of my life and never tired of it.

If you really want to pimp your Mushroom Soup, use any combination of fancy mushrooms that you can get your hands on at the store. Mushroom nirvana will be yours. For more soupy nirvana there's always The KETO Soup Bowl Cookbook at http://carriebrown.com/keto-soup-bowl-cookbook.

SIDE DISH: Spiced Pumpkin Soup

Prep time: 5 mins | Cook time: 5 mins | Total time: 10mins | Serves: 4 - 6

3 cups / 1 ½ pints chicken stock

30 oz. / 840g (2 cans) pumpkin (nothing else added, just schmushed pumpkin)

1 tsp. fresh chopped sage

1 tsp. fresh chopped rosemary

½ tsp. sea salt

¼ tsp. white pepper

¼ tsp. nutmeg

¼ cup / 2 fl oz. heavy (double) cream

1 oz. / 30g butter

½ tsp. guar gum

In a large pan, heat the stock and pumpkin over a medium heat until just beginning to boil.

Remove from the heat and transfer to a blender. Blend it on high. A lot.

Add the sage, rosemary, sea salt, pepper, nutmeg, cream, and butter.

Blend it a lot more. Then, if you want it really smooth and creamy, blend it just a little bit more.

Turn the blender to low, and slowly tap the guar gum through the opening in the lid. Blend for 5 seconds.

~~~~~~

This must be the fastest soup in history. If you have canned pumpkin, stock and a bunch of seasonings on hand, you can have a fantastically warming, filling bowl ready in 10 minutes. GO, pumpkin! If you prefer to use fresh pumpkin, go ahead. Just don't ask me how big a pumpkin you need or how to do it. I have never touched a real, live pumpkin IN MY LIFE. True story.

In England, we think pumpkins are strange, orange, grooved globes that Americans cut faces into for Halloween. I'm not even sure we think they're edible. OK, maybe things have changed since I wandered off westwards over a decade ago, but certainly, when I was a nipper, pumpkins were what Cinderella rode to the ball in, not something you'd eat.

However, you asked for Pumpkin Soup and I am here to serve. There are more awesome soups in The KETO Soup Bowl Cookbook at http://www.carriebrown.com/keto-soup-bowl-cookbook.

SIDE DISH: Green Bean Casserole Soup

Prep time: 10 mins | Cook time: 30 mins | Total time: 40 mins | Serves: 4 - 6

1 lb. / 450g trimmed green beans, chopped into 1" pieces

10 oz. / 280g onion, roughly chopped

2 TBSP coconut oil

8 oz. / 225g mushrooms, roughly chopped

2 cups /1 pint chicken stock

½ cup / 4 fl oz. heavy (double) cream

1 tsp. sea salt

Ground black pepper to taste

¼ tsp. celery salt

½ tsp. konjac flour (glucomannan powder)

½ tsp. guar gum

Steam the green beans until just crisp-tender. Drain well – because no one likes soggy beans.

Meanwhile, sauté the onion in the coconut oil for about 10 minutes, until transparent. Add the mushrooms and sauté for a further 5 minutes.

Add the stock, cream, sea salt, pepper, and celery salt, bring to the boil, and cook for 1 minute.

Transfer the soup to the blender and blend briefly on the lowest speed so that the onion and mushrooms stay in pieces.

With the blender still on low, slowly tap the konjac flour and then the guar gum through the opening in the lid. Blend for 5 seconds.

Pour the soup back into the pan and stir in the reserved green beans.

~~~~~~

I thought it would be fun to make a soup version of America's beloved Green Bean Casserole that you can enjoy all year round. The onions aren't crispy, and it's all made from scratch, but it tastes delicious. ☺ Have a cup with your roast turkey!

For more fantastic soup recipes check out the The KETO Soup Bowl Cookbook at http://carriebrown.com/keto-soup-bowl-cookbook. 40 fat-burning, health-boosting bowls of deliciousness. Lasagna Soup, anyone? Bacon and Brussels Sprouts Chowder? How about some Sausage and Kale Soup? Or maybe Creamy Chicken and Mushroom? It's all in there!

SIDE DISH: Sour Cream and Chive Biscuits / Scones

Prep time: 10 mins | Cook time: 15 mins | Total time: 25 mins | Serves: 12

15 oz. / 420g almond flour (ground almonds)

4 tsp. baking powder

1 tsp. baking soda

2 tsp. xanthan gum

½ tsp. salt

6 oz. / 170g unsalted butter, cold

1 egg

½ cup sour cream

1 TBSP cold water

½ oz. fresh chives, chopped

6 oz. / 170g feta cheese, chopped into small pieces

Beaten egg to glaze

Paprika

Preheat oven to 375°F.

Place almond flour, baking powder, baking soda, xanthan gum, salt, and cold butter into a food processor and pulse just until it resembles breadcrumbs. Do not over process!

Turn into a mixing bowl. Add the egg, sour cream, water, chives, and feta cheese and mix just enough to form a rough, soft dough.

Turn onto a board and knead about 10 times until the dough comes together. It will be shaggy.

Flatten the dough lightly with your hand until it is a 1" thick square. Cut into 2" squares with a sharp knife. Place biscuits on a baking sheet, brush with beaten egg, and sprinkle with paprika.

Bake in the center of the oven for 12 - 15 minutes until golden brown.

~~~~~~

"SHUT UP! These are so delicious…I mean SO DELICIOUS!!! I haven't had a real biscuit in a looooong time, but these taste better than anything I remember…and what surprised me the most is the moist, light texture which I never expect when baking with almond flour, etc.…they are just melt in your mouth delicious!" - Anna

"OMG! Carrie, these biscuits are absolutely amazing. Taste and texture are phenomenal." – Nina

SIDE DISH: Creamy Sausage Pecan Stuffing

Prep time: 15 mins | Cook time: 1 hour | Total time: 1 hour 15 mins | Serves 10 – 12

1 lb. / 450g ground pork (sausage meat)

1 lb. / 450g cauliflower rice (cauliflower processed to resemble rice)

1 ½ TBSP dried sage

4 TBSP red wine vinegar

4 oz. / 110g cream cheese

5 oz. / 140g onion, finely chopped

6 oz. / 170g celery, finely chopped

1 TBSP coconut oil

5 oz. / 140g mushrooms, finely chopped

4 oz. / 110g pecans, roughly chopped

Sea salt and pepper to taste

3 eggs, beaten

Preheat oven to 350°F.

Cook the sausage in a pan over medium heat, breaking up the meat into very small pieces as it cooks. Once the sausage is no longer pink, add the riced cauliflower, dried sage, and red wine vinegar and stir well. Continue cooking, stirring frequently, until the cauliflower is very soft – about 20 minutes. Once the cauliflower is very soft, add the cream cheese to the pork mixture and stir well until the cream cheese is completely melted and mixed through.

Meanwhile, in a separate pan, sauté the onion and celery in the coconut oil for 10 minutes until starting to soften, then add the mushrooms and pecans and sauté for a further 5 minutes. Remove pork mixture from the heat, add the sautéed vegetables, mix well, and season to taste with sea salt and ground black pepper. Add the beaten eggs and mix well.

Put the stuffing into a casserole dish and bake in the center of the oven for 30 minutes until the top is nicely browned.

~~~~~~

"This is truly a traditional stuffing replacement. It's full of the flavors of the season. I also love it because it won't get soggy!" – Sara

"This stuffing is HEAVENLY. I am afraid if I make this for Thanksgiving dinner I will hoard it and not share with the rest of my family, its that's good!" – Mic

SIDE DISH: Wild Leek and Hazelnut Stuffing

Prep time: 15 mins | Cook time: 1 hour | Total time: 1 hour 15 mins | Serves 10 - 12

2 lb. / 900g cauliflower rice (cauliflower processed to resemble rice)

1 cup / 8 fl oz. white cooking wine

1 TBSP dried thyme

1 ½ tsp. sea salt

Ground black pepper to taste

1 TBSP avocado oil

12 oz. / 340g leeks, sliced and chopped

7 oz. / 195g wild mushrooms, roughly chopped (what assortment of wild mushrooms you like)

3 TBSP lemon juice

4 oz. / 110g cream cheese

6 oz. / 110g toasted hazelnuts, roughly chopped

3 eggs, beaten

Preheat oven to 350°F.

Put the cauliflower rice in a large pan, add the white wine, dried thyme, sea salt, and black pepper and stir well. Cook over a medium heat, stirring frequently, until the cauliflower is very soft – about 20 minutes.

Meanwhile, in a separate pan, sauté the leeks in the avocado oil over medium heat for about 10 minutes until softened, then add the mushrooms and sauté for a further 5 minutes.

Once the cauliflower is very soft, remove pan from the heat. Add the lemon juice and cream cheese to the cauliflower and stir well until the cream cheese is completely melted and mixed through. Add the sautéed vegetables and the toasted hazelnuts to the cauliflower and mix well. Add the beaten eggs and stir until completely combined. Put the stuffing into a casserole dish and bake in the center of the oven for 40 minutes until the top is nicely browned. Just make sure you don't burn the nuts. Burnt nuts are a no-no.

~~~~~~

This stuffing involves three of my favorite ingredients: leeks, mushrooms, and hazelnuts. ALL IN THE SAME DISH. Just typing this recipe out is making me happy, but it's quite possible that's because I am eating a plate of this stuffing along with a glass of Eggnog *at this very moment*.

Never tried leeks? Don't normally eat hazelnuts? It's the holidays: Now's the time!

SIDE DISH: I Can't Believe it's Not Mash

Prep time: 5 mins | Cook time: 15 mins | Total time: 20 mins | Serves: 4

½ lb. / 225g celeriac (celery root), peeled and chopped into even-sized pieces

1 lb. / 450g cauliflower, cut into florets

2 oz. / 55g cream cheese

1 oz. / 30g butter

Sea salt and ground black pepper to taste

Boil the celeriac in water over a medium heat until tender – about 12 minutes – and drain well.

Meanwhile, steam the cauliflower until soft – about 15 minutes – and drain well.

Put the cooked vegetables in a food processor with the cream cheese, butter, sea salt, and pepper and blend until smooth. PS. You could use a masher to do the mashin', but it just doesn't give the same result. Sad but true.

~~~~~~

AH, *mashed potatoes*. Just typing that gave me minor heart palpitations. Unfortunately, when consumed, it also makes my blood sugar skyrocket, which is not nearly so appealing as a little bit of heart fluttering. Darn. The beloved mash just had to go. Sob.

I think most people who have decided to forego the once-staple spud on their plates have come across, if not tried, using cauliflower as a substitute for the world's favorite starchy mash. You can find mashed cauliflower recipes from one end of the online super-highway to the other. But every recipe I've tried for cauliflower mash has missed the mark, mainly in the texture department. No matter what I've tried, it has always come out on the wet and sloppy side. I've seen pictures of stiff cauliflower mash, but never managed to get that result myself. Most of the recipes I've seen add other – usually dairy – ingredients in an attempt to amp up the flavor and get that infamous smooth, creamy texture, but the resultant mash has just been looser and wetter than ever. Maybe it's just me, but wet mash just doesn't make my mouth happy. Plus, cauliflower isn't the most flavorful fellow in the vegetable patch. Convinced that you deserve some awesome mash, I fiddled around with various things until I settled on the humble – and extraordinarily ugly – celeriac (celery root). When cooked, celeriac has this gloriously velvety texture and ability to absorb {some} moisture, so it thickens up the mashed cauliflower beautifully, giving that oh-so-familiar mashed potato feel. Cream cheese gives extra body, and butter adds flavor. All-in-all, this is the closest thing to mashed potatoes in terms of taste and texture I have ever eaten. WINNING. (PS. Celeriac has half the net carbs of almonds. Just sayin').

Another mash recipe: http://carriebrown.com/keto-sides-salads-cookbook.

SIDE DISH: Brussels Sprouts with Almonds and Cranberries

Prep time: 10 mins | Cook time: 30 mins | Total time: 40 mins | Serves: 2 - 4

4 TBSP coconut or avocado oil

1 lb. / 450g Brussels Sprouts

4 oz. / 110g cabbage, shredded

8 oz. / 225g cauliflower florets

1 ½ oz. slivered, toasted almonds

2 oz. / 55g unsweetened dried cranberries

2 TBSP fresh parsley, finely chopped

½ tsp. sea salt

Ground black pepper to taste

Preheat oven to 350˚F. As it is heating, melt 2 TBSP of the oil in a roasting pan in the oven.

Trim the sprouts, cut them in half, and carefully toss them in the hot coconut oil. Roast them in the oven for 20 minutes – they will be just turning golden brown.

Meanwhile, pulse the cabbage and cauliflower florets in a food processor until they resemble very coarse breadcrumbs. Do not over-process! About 15 pulses should be enough.

Melt the other 2 TBSP of the coconut oil in a large skillet, add the processed cabbage and cauliflower, and sauté for about 4 minutes until the cauliflower is just starting to color.

Add the almonds, cranberries, parsley, sea salt, and pepper and mix together thoroughly.

Carefully remove the sprouts from the oven and add them to the skillet, mixing them through the other veggies.

~~~~~~

I love Brussel Sprouts; they remind me of Christmas. We ate them frequently at home in England, but I remember them best for being part of our slap-up Christmas Dinner every December 25th. Roast turkey, mini sausages wrapped in bacon and roasted in the turkey juices, roast potatoes, mashed potatoes, roast parsnips, carrots, all covered in lashings of meaty gravy. And Brussels sprouts. There was another veggie in the mix too, but for reasons that I've never quite been able to put my finger on, memories of the Brussels Sprouts crowd out the rest.

This Brussels recipe is as festive as I could make it. Christmas in a serving dish. Happy Holidays!

For more scrumptious sides: http://carriebrown.com/keto-sides-salads-cookbook.

SIDE DISH: Swiss Baked Broccoli

Prep time: 5 mins | Cook time: 35 mins | Total time: 40 mins | Serves: 4

1 lb. / 450g cauliflower florets

1 lb. / 450g broccoli florets

¾ cup / 6 fl oz. chicken stock

½ tsp. sea salt

Ground black pepper to taste

6 oz. / 170g Swiss cheese, grated

Preheat oven to 375˚F.

Place the cauliflower and stock in a pan over medium heat, bring to the boil, reduce heat to a simmer, cover, and cook for 15 minutes until the cauliflower is very soft.

Meanwhile, steam the broccoli for 10 minutes until just barely tender. Drain well.

Place the cauliflower and stock, sea salt, pepper, and 5 oz. / 140g of the Swiss cheese in a blender, and blend until smooth. Pour the cheese sauce into the pan with the drained broccoli and stir gently until completely combined.

Pour carefully into a baking dish and sprinkle the remaining 1 oz. / 30 g Swiss cheese over the broccoli and bake in the oven for 20 minutes, until the cheese is bubbling and golden.

~~~~~~

I was working on recipes for my KETO Sides and Salads Cookbook (available at http://carriebrown.com/keto-sides-salads-cookbook) when I ran a little contest on the "Carrie Brown: Life in the Sane Lane" Facebook group just to keep everyone entertained while they were waiting. One of the questions was, "I know some of you will find this hard to believe, but there are veggies that I don't like. Gasp! Name one of them!!"

One of the responses was *"Broccoli – one of my faves but I don't think you've made a recipe with it."* I realized, by Jove, she's right. Not about the not liking it part, about the not having made a broccoli recipe part. I do indeed like broccoli. I wouldn't go so far as to say that it's one of my favorites, but I'll happily gobble it up if it's there.

So here you go – a broccoli recipe. Beautiful green broccoli buried in swathes of creamy Swiss cheese sauce and baked in the oven until tender. During baking, the broccoli gets very soft, but not mushy, while the cheese sauce just gets more awesome. Is that possible?

I really think I might eat more broccoli now I get to eat it like this.

SIDE DISH: Orange Pecan Brussels and Cabbage

Prep time: 10 mins | Cook time: 10 mins | Total time: 20 mins | Serves: 4

6 oz. / 170g butter, softened

Zest of 1 orange

1 ½ tsp. orange essence

½ tsp. sea salt

Ground black pepper

3 oz. / 85g toasted pecans, finely chopped

10 oz. / 280g Brussels Sprouts, shredded

10 oz. / 280g cabbage, shredded

½ cup / 4 fl oz. water

In a bowl, mix together the butter, orange zest, orange essence, sea salt, pepper, and pecans until completely combined. It takes a little effort to bring it all together. Hang in there. This is enough for two batches of Brussels, so keep the remainder in 'fridge.

Place the Brussels, cabbage, and water in a large pan over medium-high heat and cook for about 12 - 15 minutes, until crisp-tender. You do not want soggy greens. Really, you don't.

Drain really well and return to the hot pan. Add the orange pecan butter and toss the greens well until completely coated.

~~~~~~

You may never want to eat Brussels any other way after eating this. Don't say I didn't warn you.

In the spirit of full disclosure, I am – *at this very moment* – shoveling forkfuls of this recipe into my mouth between typing sentences. I had some left over in the 'fridge after a recipe-creating-marathon earlier in the week, so when hunger struck, I yanked it out, dolloped it in a pan on the stove, warmed it up, threw some chopped ham in, and called it dinner. It is delicious. It also doesn't taste like Brussels Sprouts. Or cabbage. It tastes of oranges and toasted pecans. Oh, and this version tastes of ham. Bacon would be good, too. Lots of bacon.

I do declare that this would make a smashing lunch. Two minutes in the microwave and voila! Scrumptiousness right at your desk. No one else will want their sandwiches once the aroma of this delicious concoction wafts under their noses. Not to mention you won't be face-planting mid-afternoon like your sandwich-toting colleagues. Brussels for lunch – now there's a thing.

SIDE DISH: Cranberry Sauce

Prep time: 5 mins | Cook time: 15 mins | Total time: 20 mins | Serves: 8

Zest and juice of 1 large orange

Approx. ¾ cup / 6 fl oz. hot water (see instructions)

12 oz. / 340g fresh cranberries

8 oz. / 225g xylitol (DO **NOT** USE ERYTHRITOL!)

Put an apron on. Seriously. Cranberry juice stains like the devil.

Zest the orange straight into a pan.

Juice the orange and add enough water to make 1 cup / 8 fl oz.

Put the orange juice water, cranberries, and xylitol in the pan with the zest and stir well.

Over a high heat, bring to the boil.

Reduce the heat to a simmer and cook for 15 minutes, stirring well and often.

Remove from the heat and careful pour the sauce into a bowl.

Leave to cool completely.

Please be very careful when cooking and pouring this sauce – it gets extremely hot and would cause a burn if it comes into contact with your skin

~~~~~~

For all you lovely folks who like your Cranberry Sauce smooth, jellied and delivered in slices on your plate – it's the next recipe. If you're looking for a traditional lumpy version of Cranberry Sauce, this is the one for you.

The jellied version is slightly more convoluted to make than the lumpy version, but it's much more exciting in the long run because you get this magnificent dome of perfect, beautiful, glistening redness at the end of it. No one will believe you made it yourself. Make it the centerpiece of your holiday table and then floor them by telling them it's sugar-free to boot.

On the other hand, if you're planning on wowing your family and friends with the Vanilla Cranberry Panna Cotta (see page 83) then you'll need to make the lumpy version above.

In England we're all about the lumpy stuff. In fact, when I moved to America, I was completely confused by the jellied version. Cranberry Sauce that is the shape of a can? Whatever next.

SIDE DISH: Jellied Cranberry Sauce

Prep time: 5 mins | Cook time: 15 mins | Total time: 20 mins | Serves: 10

12 oz. / 340g fresh cranberries

1 cup / 8 fl oz. hot water

8 oz. / 225g xylitol (DO **NOT** USE ERYTHRITOL!)

Put an apron on. Seriously. Cranberry juice stains like the devil.

Put the cranberries in a pan with the hot water over a high heat and bring to the boil.

Reduce the heat to a simmer, cover with a lid – this is important! – and cook for 5 minutes.

Carefully pour the cranberries into a blender and blend on high until completely smooth.

Rinse the pan out and place a sieve over it. Push the puréed cranberries through the sieve, using a clean spatula to scrape the purée from the underside.

Add the xylitol to the cranberry purée, stir well, place over medium heat, and bring to the boil.

Reduce heat to a simmer and cook for 10 minutes, stirring well and often. If you don't stir you will end up with a lot of super thick gunk on the bottom. We don't want that.

Carefully pour the cranberry sauce into a bowl. Whatever bowl you choose is the shape the jellied cranberry sauce will become, so choose carefully. Make sure the bowl is widest at the top otherwise it will be really difficult to slide your jellied cranberry sauce out.

Leave to cool completely.

Once cold, gently press around the edge of the jelly to free it from the sides of the bowl. Put a plate upside down on the bowl and turn the bowl over so that the plate is now on the bottom.

You may need to gently push the jellied cranberry sauce to one edge of the bowl before you turn it onto the plate so that it comes out easily.

Serve as a beautiful glistening jewel on the serving plate or slice.

Please be very careful when cooking and pouring this sauce – it gets extremely hot and would cause a burn if it comes into contact with your skin

~~~~~~

"This is Delicious! I am so making this for Thanksgiving this year!" – Wren

SIDE DISH: Avocado & Walnut Salad

Prep time: 10 mins | Serves: 6 - 8

1 Butter or Bibb lettuce

1 Romaine lettuce

4 TBSP olive oil

1 ½ TBSP xylitol or erythritol

2 TBSP white wine vinegar

1TBSP finely chopped fresh parsley

¼ tsp. dried oregano

Coarse salt and ground pepper

2 avocados

2 oz. / 55g shelled walnuts, chopped into large pieces

Tear the lettuces into large pieces and place in a serving dish or bowl.

Whisk the olive oil, xylitol or erythritol, white wine vinegar, parsley, and oregano in a small bowl until completely blended and the sweetener dissolved. Season with salt and pepper to taste.

Cut the avocadoes in half lengthwise, remove the stone, peel and then slice neatly into pieces.

Add avocado pieces to the dressing and carefully turn to coat them completely. Spoon the avocado slices evenly over the bed of lettuce.

Drizzle the remaining dressing over the salad and then sprinkle the walnuts evenly on top.

~~~~~~

This salad is perfectly simple for a crazed holiday dinner state of mind. Two kinds of lettuce – one buttery and soft, one crisp and slightly bitter – plus creamy avocado pieces and crunchy walnuts all combine in every bite, held together with a slightly sweet and slightly tangy, flavorful herb dressing. Cool, refreshing, delicious.

It's the perfect accompaniment for a hearty plate of comfort food like those that adorn many a holiday table during Thanksgiving or Christmas. Quick and easy to throw together, and beautiful greens to brighten up the table.

"This has to be one of my favorite salads. I loved the avocado!" – Justin

"What a fantastic salad!! It looks as great as it tastes!" – Ramona

SIDE DISH: Celery and Cucumber Salad with Herbs

Prep time: 10 mins | Serves: 8 - 10

1½ English cucumbers, peeled, seeded, and thinly sliced crosswise (see instructions)

4 celery stalks, thinly sliced crosswise

⅓ cup coarsely chopped fresh flat-leaf parsley

⅓ cup coarsely chopped fresh mint

3 TBSP extra-virgin olive oil

Coarse salt and freshly ground black pepper

Bag of mixed salad greens

Peel the cucumbers with a peeler. Cut off the ends. Cut the whole cucumber in half crosswise. Cut each piece in half lengthwise. Run a teaspoon down the center of the cucumber to cleanly and easily remove the seeds, leaving you with hollowed out cucumber "boats." Then slice thinly crosswise.

Toss the sliced celery, sliced cucumber, chopped parsley, and mint, plus the olive oil, into a bowl and mix thoroughly.

In a shallow serving dish or platter, spread a bed of the mixed salad greens. Spoon the celery / cucumber mixture over the greens leaving the salad around the edge of the dish uncovered.

Season with salt and pepper and garnish with sprigs of parsley and mint.

~~~~~~

It's the holidays! **YES!** Let's make a ridiculously easy and delicious salad! Celery and Cucumber Salad with Herbs!

This is possibly the freshest, crunchiest, most refreshing salad. It will be a fabulous addition to your holiday menu this year. It'll make your taste buds perk right up after all that turkey and mash (for mash, see page 57). It's fast to make, with a simple flavorful dressing to give you a crisp, lively combination of flavors that your family and friends won't soon forget. Plus, it'll make your holidays healthier, so there's that.

If you're not a fan of celery then let me assure you that the sweetness of the English cucumbers and the fragrant fresh herbs perfectly even out the normally overpowering celery taste. Quick and easy to throw together, it will also withstand a wait in the 'fridge better than most salads, so it doesn't have to be a manic last-minute dish. Just add this to your holiday salad repertoire to keep things interesting.

DESSERT: Pumpkin Pie Squares

Prep time: 15 mins | Cook time: 1 hour | Total time: 1 hour 15 mins | Serves: 16

3 oz. / 85g butter

8 oz. / 225g almond flour (ground almonds)

2 oz. / 55g erythritol

15 oz. / 420g (1 can) pure unsweetened pumpkin puree

½ cup / 4 fl oz. heavy cream

½ cup / 4 fl oz. thick coconut milk (canned)

4 oz. / 110g erythritol

1 tsp. ground ginger

1 tsp. ground cinnamon

⅛ tsp. ground cloves

3 eggs, beaten

Preheat oven to 375°F. Line a 9" square tin with parchment paper and spray lightly with coconut or avocado oil.

In a pan, melt the butter over very low heat. Remove from the heat, stir in the almond flour and erythritol, and mix until completely combined.

Tip the almond flour mixture into the tin and spread evenly across the bottom, pressing into all the corners and edges. I find the bottom of a glass is helpful in the endeavor to get flat and even. Bake the crust in the center of the oven for 12 minutes.

Meanwhile, place the pumpkin puree, cream, coconut milk, erythritol, ginger, cinnamon, cloves, and beaten eggs into a bowl and mix well until completely combined.

Carefully remove the crust from the oven and reduce the heat to 350°F. Pour the pumpkin mixture over the crust and spread out to make sure it is even.

Return to the oven and bake in the center for 50 minutes until the pumpkin custard is set, firm to the touch, and a knife inserted in the middle comes out clean.

~~~~~~

Top Tip: Baking in a square tin and cutting into squares makes it super easy to serve a large crowd.

"It's impossible to believe this isn't traditional pumpkin pie." – Mrs. Bush

DESSERT: Pecan Pie

Prep time: 15 mins | Cook time: 1 hour | Total time: 1 hour 15 mins | Serves: 10 - 12

6 oz. / 170g almond flour (ground almonds)

1 oz. / 30g coconut flour

1 ½ oz. / 45g erythritol

¼ tsp. konjac flour / glucomannan powder

1 oz. / 30g butter, melted

2 eggs, beaten

6 oz. 170g butter

3 oz. / 85g erythritol

⅓ cup / 2 ½ fl oz. heavy cream

⅓ cup / 2 ½ fl oz. thick coconut milk (canned)

1 oz. / 30g vegetable glycerin

1 tsp. vanilla extract

2 eggs, beaten

½ tsp. guar gum

5 oz. / 140g pecan halves

Preheat oven to 325˚F. Mix the almond flour, coconut flour, erythritol, and konjac flour together in a bowl. Add the 1 oz. / 30g melted butter and 2 beaten eggs and mix well. Press crust into a 9" tart pan sprayed with coconut or avocado oil. Prick crust with a fork. Place the tart tin onto a baking sheet and bake in the center of the oven for 15 minutes and then remove.

Meanwhile, melt the 6 oz. / 170g butter over a high heat just until it starts to brown. Immediately remove pan from the heat and add the 3 oz. / 85g erythritol, heavy cream, thick coconut milk, and glycerin and whisk well until smooth. Leave to cool.

To the cooled butter mixture, add the vanilla extract and beaten eggs. While whisking the mixture with one hand, gently and slowly shake the guar gum into the liquid with the other hand. Add the pecans and stir well. Carefully pour the mixture into the crust shell. The baking sheet makes it much easier to transport a tart crust full of liquidy filling.

Return to the center of the oven and bake for 45 minutes until set. If the crust looks like it is getting too dark before the end of the baking time, carefully lay a piece of foil loosely over the top of the tart.

DESSERT: Chocolate Cream Tart

Prep time: 20 mins | Cook time: 15 mins | Total time: 35 mins | Serves: 12

2 ½ oz. / 70g unsalted butter, melted

2 oz. / 55g erythritol

4 oz. / 110g almond flour (ground almonds)

1 oz. / 30g cocoa powder, sifted

½ cup / 4 fl oz. heavy cream

½ cup / 4 fl oz. thick coconut milk (canned)

½ cup / 4 fl oz. almond milk

2 oz. / 55g butter

1 oz. / 30g cocoa powder, sifted

3 oz. / 85g erythritol

½ tsp. espresso powder

4 egg yolks

3 oz. / 85g 100% unsweetened chocolate (NOT cocoa powder), finely chopped

To the melted unsalted butter add the 2 oz. / 55g erythritol, almond flour, and 1 oz. / 30g sifted cocoa powder and mix until completely combined. Press into a 9" loose bottomed tart tin – whatever shape you have. Press the crust into the corners, edges, and up the sides.

Place the cream, coconut milk, almond milk, butter, 1 oz. / 30g sifted cocoa powder, erythritol, and espresso powder into a pan and whisk well over a medium heat until the mixture starts to steam.

Whisk the egg yolks in a small bowl. While still whisking the egg yolks, slowly add 1 cup / 8 fl oz. of the hot chocolate cream mixture from the pan to the bowl with the yolks. Pour the egg mixture back into the pan and stir constantly for 10 - 12 minutes while the custard thickens. Pour the thickened custard through a fine mesh sieve into a clean bowl, add the finely chopped chocolate, and stir until the chocolate is completely melted and mixed in.

Pour the chocolate custard into the chocolate crust and cool completely before putting in the 'fridge to set for several hours.

Whip 1 cup / 8 fl oz. heavy cream with 2 TBSP erythritol until you have soft peaks. Spread the cream over the cold tart and decorate with chocolate shavings, chocolate drizzle, or just pile the cream high and leave it naked in all its white, creamy gorgeousness.

DESSERT: Eggnog Ice Cream

Prep time: 15 mins | Cook time: 15 mins | Total time: 30 mins + freezing | Serves: 10 - 12

4 ½ oz. / 125g xylitol (DO **NOT** USE ERYTHRITOL!)

½ tsp. guar gum

1 tsp. sea salt

1 cup / 8 fl oz. almond milk

6 egg yolks

1 cup / 8 fl oz. heavy cream

1 cup / 8 fl oz. thick coconut milk (canned)

1 ½ tsp. ground nutmeg

2 TBSP rum

2 tsp. vanilla extract

Mix the xylitol, guar gum, and sea salt together well in a pan. Add the almond milk, whisk well, and warm over a medium heat until it just starts to steam.

Whisk the egg yolks in a small bowl. While still whisking the egg yolks, slowly add 1 cup / 8 fl oz. of the almond milk mixture from the pan into the bowl with the yolks. Pour the egg mixture back into the pan and stir constantly for 10 - 12 minutes while the custard thickens. Pour the thickened custard through a fine mesh sieve into a clean bowl. Add the cream, coconut milk, ground nutmeg, rum, and vanilla extract and stir well.

Cover the bowl and place in the 'fridge for at least 8 hours, preferably overnight or for several days. It gets better the longer you chill it.

Churn the ice cream in your churner according to the manufacturer's instructions. It typically takes between 20 - 30 minutes to freeze. Once the ice cream has frozen to a soft-serve consistency, quickly transfer it from the churning bowl into your pre-chilled container and place in the freezer for at least 8 hours, preferably overnight.

~~~~~~

Making great low carb ice cream is an art. Having a great recipe is crucial, but there are a bunch of other things that will help make your ice cream even better. So much so that I wrote a whole cookbook just on ice creams. For the whole scoop (ha! ha!), all the tips and tricks plus 52 amazing recipes, check out the The KETO Ice Cream Scoop Cookbook:

http://carriebrown.com/keto-ice-cream-scoop-cookbook

DESSERT: Orange Spice Ice Cream (*Low Carb)

Prep time: 15 mins | Cook time: 10 mins | Total time: 25 mins + freezing | Serves: 10 - 12

½ cup / 4 fl oz. heavy (double) cream

1 tsp. sea salt

5 ¼ oz. / 150g xylitol (DO **NOT** USE ERYTHRITOL!)

Zest ½ orange

10 oz. / 280g orange flesh, peeled

1 ½ cups / 12 fl oz. thick coconut milk

2 tsp. ground coriander

½ tsp. ground cloves

½ tsp. vanilla extract

½ cup / 4 fl oz. pasteurized egg whites

½ tsp. guar gum

Warm the cream, sea salt, and xylitol in a pan until it just starts to boil. Remove from heat, zest the orange directly into the cream, stir, cover, and steep for an hour.

Sieve the orange cream to remove the orange zest. Do not leave the orange zest in! It makes the ice cream bitter. Ignore this at your peril.

Place the orange-infused cream, orange flesh, thick coconut milk, ground coriander, ground cloves, vanilla extract, and egg whites in the blender and blend for 10 seconds.

Turn the blender to low speed and, while the blender is running, add the guar gum through the opening in the lid and blend for 5 seconds. Do not over blend.

Pour the ice cream mix into a bowl, cover, and place in the 'fridge for at least 8 hours, preferably overnight.

Churn the ice cream in your churner according to the manufacturer's instructions. It typically takes between 20 - 30 minutes to freeze. Once the ice cream has frozen to a soft-serve consistency, quickly transfer it from the churning bowl into your pre-chilled container and place in the freezer for at least 8 hours, preferably overnight.

~~~~~~

This tastes like Christmas. Or Thanksgiving. I still get confused by the two. They both involve turkey, poinsettias, and loads of people gobbling up loads of food. It's an easy mistake.

DESSERT: Vanilla Cranberry Panna Cotta

Prep time: 10 mins | Cook time: 5 mins | Total time: 15 mins | Serves: 4 - 6

2 cups / 16 fl oz. heavy cream

2 oz. / 55g erythritol

1 vanilla bean OR 2 tsp. vanilla extract

3 TBSP cold water

2 tsp. powdered gelatin

1 cup / 8 fl oz. whole berry cranberry sauce (see page 65)

Put the cream and erythritol in a pan on medium heat, stirring until the erythritol has completely dissolved and then turn the heat off.

Split the vanilla bean lengthwise with a sharp knife and scrape the seeds out. Add both the seeds and the pod to the pan with the warm cream and let steep for 30 minutes. If you are using vanilla extract instead of a pod, add the vanilla extract and proceed to the next step. If you are using a pod, rewarm the cream after 30 minutes of steeping and then proceed to the next step.

Put the cold water in a medium sized bowl (preferably one with a pouring lip, like a pancake bowl) and sprinkle the powdered gelatin evenly over the surface. Leave the gelatin to soften for 5 minutes.

Place a fine mesh sieve over the bowl with the softened gelatin in and pour the warm cream through the sieve to catch the vanilla pod and any stray pieces of fiber that got into the cream with the seeds. Remove the sieve and stir the cream mixture until the gelatin is fully dissolved.

Carefully pour the panna cotta into your pretty holiday glasses. Put the glasses on a plate and place the plate in the 'fridge. The plate just allows you to carry the glasses steadier and move them all at once. Leave in the 'fridge for at least 4 hours to set.

Just prior to serving, warm the whole berry cranberry sauce gently in a pan to melt it and stir in 1 TBSP water. Remove from the heat and leave to get cold.

Remove the glasses of panna cotta from the 'fridge and carefully spoon cranberry sauce into each glass.

Serve after dinner with a plate of "Sugar" Cookies (page 85) and then sit back and bask in the barrage of "Wows!" that will run around the table. Swoon.

~~~~~~

This can be made up to two days in advance if covered with plastic wrap and stored in the 'fridge.

DESSERT: "Sugar" Cookies

Prep time: 15 mins | Cook time: 10 mins | Total time: 25 mins | Serves: 30

5 oz. / 140g butter, softened

6 oz. / 170g xylitol

2 tsp. baking powder

1 tsp. xanthan gum

1/4 tsp. sea salt

1 tsp. vanilla extract

1 TBSP almond milk

1 egg

8 oz. / 225g almond flour (ground almonds)

1 oz. / 28g coconut flour

1 TBSP konjac flour / glucomannan powder

Place the softened butter, xylitol, baking powder, xanthan gum, and sea salt in a mixing bowl and cream together with a hand or stand mixer until light and fluffy. Add the vanilla, almond milk, and egg and mix well until completely combined.

In a separate bowl place the almond flour (ground almonds), coconut flour, konjac flour and mix well.

Add half of the flours into the butter mixture with the mixer, then add the rest of the flour with a spatula until it is completely incorporated into a dough. Wrap the dough in plastic wrap or place in a Ziploc bag and put in the 'fridge for at least two hours to become firm.

Preheat the oven to 350˚F. Take the dough out of the 'fridge and carefully roll out to 1/8" – 1/4" thick using a little almond flour to stop it sticking to the work surface or the rolling pin.

Use the cutter of your choice to cut out the dough. I used a 2" round plain cutter. Since it's the holidays you might just want to do something more fun. DO IT!! Whatever cutter you use, place the cookies on a baking sheet 1" apart.

Bake in the center of the oven for 10 - 12 minutes – until they're just starting to brown a little.

Remove from the oven and leave on the tray until the cookies have firmed up enough to move them without breaking or getting misshapen. Resist the temptation to touch them!

Using a flat spatula, move the cookies carefully onto a cooling rack to cool completely.

www.carriebrown.com

DESSERT: Chocolate Rum Truffles

Prep time: 15 mins | Cook time: 2 mins | Total time: 17 mins + 2 hours cooling | Serves: 16

4 oz. / 110g 100% unsweetened dark chocolate (NOT cocoa powder)

½ cup / 4 fl oz. heavy cream

1 tsp. rum

2 TBSP vegetable glycerin

3 TBSP xylitol or erythritol

4 oz. / 110g unsweetened cocoa powder (this is for rolling, you won't use all this)

Finely chop the chocolate and place in a bowl.

Put the cream, rum, vegetable glycerin, and xylitol or erythritol in a pan, and stir well over medium heat. Heat until the cream just barely begins to boil. As soon as you see the first bubbles break the surface, immediately pour the cream over the chopped chocolate in the bowl and stir using a whisk until the chocolate is completely melted and you have a thick, glossy, utterly glorious bowl of chocolate ganache – this last part will only take about 15 seconds.

Press plastic wrap onto the surface of the chocolate and leave to cool. The plastic wrap stops a skin forming. Once cooled, place in the 'fridge for an hour to firm up.

Once firm enough to roll, remove from the 'fridge and prepare to get a little chocolate-y. That's code for "put an apron on." Sieve the cocoa powder into a bowl and have a clean plate ready to receive the finished truffles.

Using a teaspoon, scoop some truffle mix out of the bowl and very quickly roll into a ball between the palms of your hands. Drop the truffle into the bowl of cocoa powder and gently toss to coat – or use a large spoon to gently toss cocoa powder over the truffle. The heat from your hands will be enough to just melt the outside of the truffle, so that the cocoa powder sticks to the surface without you having to perform an additional step of rolling in liquid chocolate before tossing in cocoa powder. However, be quick when you roll the truffles into a ball so that they don't melt too much or you'll end up with an almighty mess on your hands. It is definitely easier (and faster) if you have another pair of hands to do the tossing-in-the-cocoa-powder part, but it's perfectly possible to achieve if it's just you, yourself, and you.

Gentle drop the truffles into mini paper cups or onto a serving dish.

~~~~~~

The truffle mix can be made several days in advance if covered with plastic wrap and stored in the 'fridge. Remove from 'fridge an hour before rolling.

BEVERAGE: Eggnog

Prep time: 10 mins | Cook time: 15 mins | Total time: 25 mins | Serves: 6 - 8

4 eggs

2 ½ oz. / 70g erythritol

1 ½ cups / 12 fl oz. heavy cream

1 ½ cups / 12 fl oz. almond milk

1 tsp. ground nutmeg

¼ cup / 2 fl oz. rum

2 TBSP xylitol (DO NOT USE ERYTHRITOL!)

Separate the eggs – put the whites in a large bowl and the yolks in a small bowl.

Put the erythritol, cream, and almond milk in a pan over medium heat and stir well until the erythritol has all dissolved. Leave it to heat just until it is steaming.

Whisk the egg yolks in the small bowl. While still whisking the egg yolks, slowly add 1 cup / 8 fl oz. of the hot cream mixture from the pan to the bowl with the yolks.

Pour the egg mixture back into the pan of cream and stir constantly for 10 - 12 minutes while the custard thickens. Pour the thickened custard through a fine mesh sieve into a clean bowl, add the nutmeg and rum, and stir well. Leave to cool.

Once the egg cream mixture is cooled, whip the egg whites in the large bowl using a hand or stand mixer until they form soft peaks. While still whipping the egg whites, gradually add the xylitol and then whip until stiff peaks form.

By hand, gently whisk the stiff egg whites into the cool egg custard. Pour the eggnog into glasses and sprinkle ground nutmeg on the top.

~~~~~~

So what's the deal with this fine mesh sieve you keep seeing pop up everywhere in recipes? I thought you'd never ask.

If you want little pieces of egg – or anything else for that matter – unexpectedly swimming up as someone slurps on their glass of silky-smooth eggnog gloriousness then go ahead and forget the whole sieving part. But I urge you not to go that route because for 10 seconds of extra effort you will have *perfect* eggnog instead of possibly-lumpy eggnog.

Just another little trick that will earn you your well-deserved title of Kitchen God(dess).

BEVERAGE: Pomegranate Iced Green Tea with Lemon

½ cup / 4 fl oz. water brewed with 4 green tea bags, left to get cold
1 TBSP lemon juice
1½ TBSP unsweetened pomegranate juice
¼ tsp. ginger extract
2 TBSP erythritol (or sweetener of choice)

Add the cold brewed green tea, lemon juice, pomegranate juice, ginger extract, and sweetener into a jug and stir vigorously until erythritol is dissolved.

Pour into an ice-filled glass and garnish with a lemon slice and pomegranate seeds.

BEVERAGE: Cosmo

6 tsp. pure 100% unsweetened cranberry juice
5 TBSP water
2 TBSP lime juice
¼ tsp. orange extract
5 tsp. erythritol or to taste (or sweetener of choice)
crushed ice
cranberries, orange zest to serve

Add all liquid ingredients to a jug and stir vigorously until sweetener is dissolved. Pour into two glasses over crushed ice and garnish each with cranberries and thin strips of orange zest.

For an entire collection of beverages including lattes, hot chocolates, frappes, mocktails, teas, infused waters, soda, and more check out the 101 KETO Beverages Cookbook:
www.carriebrown.com/drink-smarter-beverages-e-cookbook

BEVERAGE: Chai Tea Latte

1 cup / 8 fl oz. 175°F water
1 tsp. ground cinnamon
¼ tsp. ground allspice
½ tsp. ground ginger
2 teabags black tea
1 TBSP erythritol (or sweetener of choice)
1 cup / 8 fl oz. nut milk of your choice
2 TBSP thick coconut milk (canned)

Boil the water in a small pan. Turn off the heat and add the cinnamon, allspice, ginger, and tea bags, and steep for 4 minutes.

Pour into cup and add sweetener to taste.

Heat the milk and the thick coconut milk until warm (not boiling) and froth with a hand frother. Pour frothed milk into brew and sprinkle with ground cinnamon.

BEVERAGE: Creamy Peppermint Hot Chocolate

1 cup / 8 fl oz. unsweetened almond milk
¼ cup thick coconut milk
1 tsp. peppermint extract
2 TBSP xylitol or erythritol (or sweetener of choice)
pinch of sea salt
1 oz. / 30g 100% unsweetened chocolate, chopped
spoonful of whipped cream
grated unsweetened chocolate to sprinkle

Place the milks, peppermint, sweetener, and sea salt in a pan over medium heat.

As it starts to steam turn off the heat and add the chopped chocolate, stirring until completely melted and mixed through.

While it is still in the pan, whisk the hot chocolate using a handheld frother or immersion blender.

Pour into mug, add a spoonful of whipped cream, and sprinkle grated chocolate over the top.

TURKEY LEFTOVERS: Turkey Tarragon Baked Eggs

Prep time: 5 mins | Cook time: 15 mins | Total time: 20 mins | Serves: 2

Coconut or avocado oil spray

4 TBSP heavy cream

4 oz. / 110g chopped cooked turkey

2 tsp fresh tarragon, chopped

4 eggs

Black pepper

8 oz. / 225g mushrooms, sliced

Preheat oven to 350°F. Spray 2 ramekin dishes with oil and place dishes in a baking pan with water half way up the outside of the ramekins.

Put 2 TBSP cream in the bottom of each dish and then place turkey on top of the cream and then bake for 5 minutes.

Carefully pull oven shelf out half way and sprinkle the fresh tarragon over the turkey. Crack 2 eggs into each dish and season with ground black pepper.

Carefully push oven shelf back into the oven and bake for 12 - 15 minutes until eggs are just cooked.

During the last 4 minutes while the eggs are cooking, gently sauté the sliced mushrooms until just starting to color.

Serve mushrooms alongside the dishes of eggs.

~~~~~~

It's always been a mystery to me whether to write new turkey recipes around the holidays so that people have new ideas for using up all that leftover bird, or whether the sight of yet another turkey recipe makes people's eyes glaze over. Brian over at www.ketovangelist.com persuaded me it was the former, so here we are. You can thank him later.

On another note, yes, I love tarragon. But, as it happens, it also goes spectacularly well with turkey – something that you may not have been aware of up to this point in your life.

Tender turkey, a splash of cream, and a couple of eggs seemed like it would make a pretty decent breakfast, and although turkey and eggs somehow don't spring to mind as an obvious combination, the tarragon totally tied it all together. You're welcome.

TURKEY LEFTOVERS: Sunshine Turkey Scramble

Prep time: 5 mins | Cook time: 15 mins | Total time: 20 mins | Serves: 1 – 2

1 TBSP coconut oil

6 oz. / 140g finely chopped or minced cooked turkey

½ small onion, finely chopped

½ medium orange, peeled and chopped into pieces (see notes* below)

3 eggs

2 TBSP water

Sea salt and pepper to season

1 TBSP dried sage

Handfuls of fresh spinach

In a skillet (frying pan), sauté the onion in the coconut oil for 2 minutes, and then add the chopped cooked turkey and stir together.

Continue sautéing the meat and onions, stirring regularly, until the turkey is lightly browned.

Add the orange pieces, mix, and then reduce the heat.

In a small bowl, whisk the eggs, water, salt, pepper, and sage together well. Add the egg mixture to the pan and mix quickly into the meat. Continue to scramble the eggs, stirring constantly.

Once the eggs are cooked to your liking, remove from the heat and serve on a large bed of fresh spinach.

~~~~~~

Amongst other things, oranges scream "Christmas!" to me, although I'm not entirely sure why. And, while oranges in your eggs might seem like an unusual choice, the idea came to me while I was brunching with a friend a while back. I ordered what was essentially an omelet with ham, cheese, and spinach – but with a hazelnut and orange dressing that had a whole pile of orange segments in it. And I thought, "Well. If you can put orange segments in a dressing and slather it all over your omelet, it stands to reason that oranges and eggs go, and therefore orange IN your scramble must be awesome." And so it was.

*I typically don't eat oranges because they're higher in sugar, but since this dish is 4g net carbs, I'll enjoy some orange-y goodness in my life, once in a blue moon. Like at the holidays. However, if you are very insulin-resistant and/or have a lot of weight to lose you will likely want to omit the oranges until you are in maintenance.

TURKEY LEFTOVERS: Turkey Pot Pie Gumbo

Prep time: 10 mins | Cook time: 30 mins | Total time: 40 mins | Serves: 4

2 ½ cups / 1 ¼ pints chicken stock

1 lb. / 450g turkey, cut into chunks

5 oz. / 140g celery, sliced

5 oz. / 140g onion, diced

6 oz. / 170g radishes, peeled and cubed

4 oz. / 110g broccoli, cut into small florets

1 lb. / 450g cauliflower, roughly chopped

½ tsp. sea salt

Ground black pepper to taste

2 oz. / 50g butter

½ tsp. konjac flour (glucomannan powder)

½ cup fresh parsley sprigs

Put the stock, turkey, celery, onion, and radishes into a large pan or stock pot and bring to the boil over medium heat. Cover, reduce heat and simmer for 10 minutes. Add broccoli and continue simmering until veggies are just tender, about 5 minutes.

Strain the stock through a sieve or colander into a large bowl, return the stock to the pan, and reserve the meat and veggies.

Add the cauliflower to the stock, bring to the boil. Cover, and simmer until the cauliflower is soft.

Carefully transfer the cauliflower and stock to the blender, add the sea salt, pepper, and butter and blend on high until very smooth.

Turn the blender to low, and slowly tap the konjac flour through the opening in the lid. Blend for 5 seconds. Add the parsley and blend for a few seconds until evenly distributed.

Pour the soup back into the pan, add the reserved meat and veggies and stir well. Heat through and serve.

~~~~~~

Like a Turkey Pot Pie, but in soup form. You could always float Cheesy Biscuits on top (http://www.ketovangelistkitchen.com/cheesy-biscuits) and have a full-on pie.

PS. There are more soups here: http://www.carriebrown.com/keto-soup-bowl-cookbook

TURKEY LEFTOVERS: Roast Turkey Casserole

Prep time: 15 mins | Cook time: 40 mins | Total time: 55 mins | Serves: 6

Coconut or avocado oil spray

1lb / 450g cooked turkey, chopped

8 oz. / 225g leeks, finely chopped

2 oz. / 55g celery, finely chopped

2 tsp dried sage

1 cup / 8 fl oz. cottage cheese

8 eggs

Lemon pepper to taste

¼ cup Parmesan cheese, grated

Preheat oven to 375˚F. Spray a 7 × 11" / 4 pint / 2 quart baking dish with oil.

In a bowl, mix the turkey, leeks, celery, sage, and cottage cheese together and then spread the turkey mixture evenly in the baking dish.

In the bowl, whisk the eggs and lemon pepper well, and then pour the eggs evenly over the turkey mixture.

Sprinkle the grated Parmesan evenly over the surface and carefully place the baking dish in the oven.

Bake for 40 minutes, until the top is golden brown and a skewer poked into the middle comes out clean.

~~~~~~

If you think you're fed up with turkey by the end of the holidays, I dare you to eat this and then still be fed up. This is another recipe that turned out to be perfect for just about every meal you can think of – breakfast – check; lunch – check; dinner – check; snack – check. It would not, however, be my first choice for dessert. It is fabulous hot right out the oven but, once cold, it can easily be transported for lunch and eaten either warm or cold. It is majorly filling. And tastes like Turkey Pot Pie without the 'pie' part.

It couldn't be easier to sling together for those days when you are just tired of cooking. Or you can make it in advance without baking it, keep it covered in the 'fridge, and then whip it out and cook it when the time is right. It's the epitome of fast, simple, easy, cheap, filling, and delicious. YUM.

TURKEY LEFTOVERS: Warm Turkey and Almond Slaw

Prep time: 1 min | Cook time: 5 mins | Total time: 6 mins | Serves: 2

1 TBSP coconut or avocado oil

6 oz. / 170g broccoli carrot slaw (I use Trader Joe's, so this is ½ packet)

1/3 cup slivered (not flaked) almonds

7 oz. / 195g chopped cooked turkey

1 tsp. dried rosemary

¼ cup / 2 fl oz. Greek yogurt (NON-FAT WILL NOT WORK!)

1 TBSP balsamic vinegar

Ground black pepper and sea salt

Heat the oil in a skillet over high heat.

Add the broccoli carrot slaw and the almonds and stir-fry for 2 minutes, stirring constantly.

Reduce the heat to medium.

Add the chopped cooked turkey, stir, and cook for 1 minute.

Add the dried rosemary and gently stir in the yogurt.

Add the balsamic vinegar, stir well, and season with salt and pepper.

~~~~~~

Top Tip: use toasted slivered almonds for extra flavor and crunch. You can buy them ready toasted or simply toast them yourself under a hot broiler (grill). Just be careful that you don't burn them as they toast real fast. Don't walk away! Don't leave them!

This is one of my One-Pan-Wonders that I am so fond of throwing together when it's just me and 3 cats around the dining table. Which is pretty much every single night. I am sure y'all have much better reasons why there are times you just want dinner to miraculously make itself. This recipe is the next best thing. Plus, almost **no dishes**. I'd hazard a guess that you've done more than your fair share of dishes over the Holidays, so an almost dish-less dinner recipe will be a very welcome reprieve. More playing and less dishes this Holiday season, that's what I say!

"This recipe is definitely a winner. So simple and delicious. Thank you for sharing!" - Kanukgurl

"Made this over the weekend. It was YUMMY! Yet another one of your recipes that my little one really enjoys!" - Mic

TURKEY LEFTOVERS: Tarragon Turkey with Leeks

Prep time: 5 mins | Cook time: 10 mins | Total time: 15 mins | Serves: 2

1 TBSP coconut or avocado oil

2 large leeks, thinly sliced

7 oz. / 200g chopped cooked turkey

4 oz. / 110g cremini mushrooms, sliced

½ cup / 4 fl oz. Greek Yogurt (DO NOT USE fat-free!)

1 TBSP fresh tarragon, chopped

1 oz. / 30g Parmesan cheese, grated

1 oz. / 28g pine nuts

Heat the oil in a skillet or frying pan, add the sliced leeks, and sauté, stirring frequently, over medium heat for 5 minutes until leeks are softened.

Stir in the turkey meat and the sliced mushrooms and continue to sauté until the mushrooms and turkey are warmed through – about 3 minutes.

Gently stir in the chopped tarragon and yogurt.

Turn the turkey mixture into a casserole dish.

Sprinkle the Parmesan cheese and pine nuts evenly over the top of the turkey.

Place under a hot broiler (grill) until the pine nuts turn golden brown. Don't walk away – you'll end up with burnt nuts! Just say no to burnt nuts!

~~~~~~

Yum. Yum. Yum. Yum. Yum.

Tarragon does something magical to turkey, you know. If I had to name my herb of the year, it would be tarragon. It totally transforms this 10-minute-dinner from turkey leftovers to terrific turkey taste-fest. As much as I love to cook, there's a lot to be said for 10-minute-dinners that are this simple, fast and tasty.

"Great tasting, quick and easy! Both husband & I liked it a lot. Would reheat well for lunches too." – Lisa

"This was absolutely first rate! Can't wait to make it again with some of my turkey leftovers after Thanksgiving!" – Andrea M

KETOVANGELIST KITCHEN RESOURCES

WEBSITE : www.ketovangelistkitchen.com

PODCAST : www.ketovangelistkitchen.com/category/podcast

FACEBOOK GROUP : www.facebook.com/groups/ketovangelistkitchen

TWITTER : www.twitter.com/KetovanKitchen

PINTEREST : www.pinterest.com/KetovanKitchen

INSTAGRAM : www.instagram.com/ketovangelistkitchen

KETOVANGELIST GENERAL KETO RESOURCES

WEBSITE : www.ketovangelistkitchen.com

PODCAST : www.ketovangelist.com/category/podcast/

FACEBOOK GROUP : www.facebook.com/groups/theketogenicathlete/

KETOGENIC ATHLETE RESOURCES

WEBSITE : www.theketogenicathlete.com

PODCAST : www.theketogenicathlete.com/category/podcast/

FACEBOOK GROUP : www.facebook.com/groups/theketogenicathlete/

WHERE TO FIND ME

www.CarrieBrown.com : delicious recipes for optimal nutrition, wellness, & fat-loss, with tips & tricks for living a super healthy, sane life, as well as travel & things to make you think.

PODCAST : www.ketovangelistkitchen.com/category/podcast

FACEBOOK (page) : www.facebook.com/CarrieBrownBlog

FACEBOOK (personal) : www.facebook.com/flamingavocado

TWITTER : www.twitter.com/CarrieBrownBlog

PINTEREST : www.pinterest.com/CarrieBrownBlog

INSTAGRAM
@carrieontrippin : day-to-day moments captured with my iPhone
@biggirlcamera : road trips, landscapes, flowers, fences, barns, & whatever else grabs my attention captured with my Big Girl Camera
@lifeinthesanelane : food, recipes, inspiration, and sane living tips
@mistermchenry : The world according to Mr. McHenry

FLICKR : www.flickr.com/photos/carrieontrippin

MEDIUM : www.medium.com/@CarrieBrownBlog : random musings on life, the Universe, & everything. Possibly rantier, more sensitive, and more controversial.

COOKBOOKS

E-cookbook / pdf versions : www.carriebrown.com/archives/31768

Print versions : www.amazon.com/author/browncarrie

I am an author, podcast co-host, recipe developer, and photographer creating useful, fun, and beautiful stuff about food, travel, and living a healthy, unmedicated, and sane life.

I use my ex-professional pastry chef talents to create scrumptious recipes to help the world eat smarter, live better, and put the 'healthy' back into healthy again. I create gluten-, grain-, sugar-, soy-free recipes for KETO, LCHF, LowCarb, Paleo, Primal, WheatBelly, Wild Diet, SANE, and other health-focused dietary approaches using real foods. What a concept! Healthy can be more delicious than you ever imagined.

This cookbook joins The KETO Ice Cream Scoop, The KETO Crockpot, The KETO Soup Bowl, 101 KETO Beverages, and KETO Sides & Salads on the culinary bookshelf. All jammed with serious whole food goodness and YUM.

When I am not making stuff up in the kitchen you'll likely find me roaring around the country shooting landscapes and otherwise exploring this amazing world that we live in. I like life better when it's real, rambunctious, and slightly irreverent.

I adore the scent of roses, have an accent like crack (apparently), and a love for people who keep on going when the going gets tough. I think leeks are the finest vegetables on earth, and fennel is pretty close behind. I can't swim.

I love living in Seattle with a couple of large cameras, a ridiculous amount of cocoa powder, and a pile of cats — Zebedee, Daisy, and Mr. McHenry. (RIP Chiko, Dougal, Penelope, and Florence). We love it here!

BREAKFASTS

APPETIZERS

ENTREES

SIDE DISHES

DESSERTS

BEVERAGES

TURKEY LEFTOVERS

Made in the USA
Lexington, KY
16 November 2017